The Healthy Compulsive

The Healthy Compulsive

*Healing Obsessive-Compulsive
Personality Disorder and Taking the
Wheel of the Driven Personality*

Gary Trosclair

ROWMAN & LITTLEFIELD
Lanham • Boulder • New York • London

Published by Rowman & Littlefield
An imprint of The Rowman & Littlefield Publishing Group, Inc.
4501 Forbes Boulevard, Suite 200, Lanham, Maryland 20706
www.rowman.com

86-90 Paul Street, London EC2A 4NE, United Kingdom

British Library Cataloguing in Publication Information Available

Library of Congress Cataloging-in-Publication Data Available

ISBN: 978-1-5381-3260-9 (cloth : alk. paper) | ISBN 978-1-5381-7630-6
(pbk. : alk. paper) | ISBN: 978-1-5381-3261-6 (electronic)

♾™ The paper used in this publication meets the minimum requirements of
American National Standard for Information Sciences—Permanence of Paper
for Printed Library Materials, ANSI/NISO Z39.48-1992.

For Carroll and Genevieve

Contents

	Preface	ix
	Introduction	1
Part I	**The Driven Personality: What It's Like and How It Got That Way**	13
Chapter 1	Identifying the Driven Personality	15
Chapter 2	How Did I Get This Way? The Tree Grows Where It Can	25
Part II	**Realizing Your Driven Potential**	41
Chapter 3	Four Steps to Becoming a Healthier Compulsive	43
Chapter 4	Step 1: Identify Your Story to Develop Insight	49
Chapter 5	Step 2: Engage Emotionally with Deeper Layers of Feeling and Parts of Yourself	59
Chapter 6	Step 3: Cultivate Meaning—Clarify Your Aspirations and Set Your Priorities	73

Chapter 7   Step 4: Take Action—Commit to Behavior
               That Honors Your Aspirations   79

**Part III   Dangers and Opportunities on the Road
               Ahead: Applying the Tools of Change
               to Fulcrum Issues**   85

Chapter 8   Body   87

Chapter 9   Time and Money   95

Chapter 10   Work and Career   105

Chapter 11   People, Partners, and Parenting   117

Chapter 12   Rest and Play   133

Chapter 13   Psychological Growth: Vicissitudes of the
               Inner Game   141

Part IV   Support for the Road Ahead   153

Chapter 14   Support for the Compulsive's Journey   155

Chapter 15   Support and Suggestions for the
               Compulsive's Partner   163

               Afterword   177

               Acknowledgments   181

               Notes   183

               Bibliography   199

               Index   207

               About the Author   217

~

Preface

When I was eighteen and a far-too-earnest young musician, my trumpet teacher advised me to chill out and read *The Inner Game of Tennis* by Timothy Gallwey.[1] Gallwey had been one point away from winning the national junior tennis championship when he choked on an easy shot and lost the match. He committed his life to figuring out why, and after extensive travels he found a Zen-flavored answer inside. He recognized two selves at work: Self 1 is the conscious, thinking ego. Self 2 is the natural, intuitive learner. We need Self 1 to get along in the world, but it shouldn't be calling the shots. It should facilitate rather than direct, but it tends to get very bossy: "Bend your elbow at a 47-degree angle, shift the weight to your left foot, get the racket head higher, No, Lower, NO, TOO MUCH—STUPID!" Gallwey concluded that when we're trying too hard Self 1 has taken over, and we become far too tense and self-critical to play our best game.

He found that when he could get Self 1 to let go and trust Self 2, his more intuitive resources, he was much more successful—at tennis and life. Becoming aware of these inner resources and using them effectively constitute the Inner Game.

Reading Gallwey was a revelation. He helped me to see that my natural energy, passion, determination, and focus, all intended to help play the Inner Game (learning, music, tennis, personal growth), got hijacked and enlisted to play the Outer Game (impressing others). This reversal made me tight and perfectionistic. Not a good setup for making music. Gallwey also helped me to see that in Self 2 there were far more aspects to me, far more helpful and rewarding aspects, than just the controlling and conscious ego I had been aware of.

But Self 1 had taken over and had a pretty tight grip on me. I was driven by perfectionism, and had lost track of my original motivation: I loved music, deeply, and I wanted to share it. But perfectionism had hijacked my love of music to prove my worth, and the deeper inspiration was pushed to the back seat.

My trumpet teacher was onto me. He could see that my will, resolve, and control could take me only so far. "Trying hard is a questionable virtue," he quipped mischievously. He was telling me, in not so many words, "Have a little faith in your natural inclinations. You play better when you get out of your own way. There's something inside of you that knows better than your ego how to make music." But who was this? Who was supposed to get out of whose way? Who should be driving?

As helpful as Gallwey's Inner Game was, in order to take back the wheel I was going to need an understanding of why Self 1 had taken over and a more detailed map of what was happening inside me.

I had already begun studying psychology at the time, and the Inner Game resonated well with some of the work I was reading, particularly that of Carl Jung. Like Gallwey, Jung had had a crisis and needed to take a deep dive into his own psyche to take back the wheel of his car. As Jung put it, "I did not live but was driven; I was a slave to my ideals."[2]

Just as Gallwey had, Jung discovered that he had two personalities. He called these personality Number 1 and personality Number 2. Number 1 dealt with the realities of getting along with people in the practical world; Number 2 was motivated by psychological growth. His take was slightly different from Gallwey's, but they were the same in one crucial respect: personality Number 1 was supposed to facilitate the aspirations of personality Number 2, not the other way around. His "ideals" should have been working to help him realize the urges toward psychological growth, the natural learning that Gallwey spoke of. But the slave had become the master.

Jung concluded that at the heart of personality Number 2, we have a compulsive urge to grow,[3] to realize our true selves and become more whole than divided. Here's where he gave me a more detailed map to follow: He found that to grow psychologically we need to consciously integrate various parts of the personality such as the Hero, with its tendency toward willful control, and the Judge, with its tendency toward perfectionism. If these parts are not integrated consciously, they can hijack the energy that comes with the urge for self-realization, and we're no longer driving; we're being driven.

I believe that this urge to psychological growth is particularly strong in people who are compulsive, and it comes with both negative and positive potential. It can be misappropriated and enlisted in projects that may seem worthwhile at first, but in the long run only lead to an endless cycle of proving worth—the Outer Game. Over decades of exploration the question has crystallized for me: will I use this energy in a healthy way, or will I get caught in the endless cycle of achievement, obsessive work, and over-the-top conscientiousness to which many compulsive people succumb?

Trying to stay on the healthy end of the spectrum has required me to create, in an ongoing way, a map of my psyche, one that extends far beyond the territory of the conscious and controlling ego. This map includes personality parts that become more helpful as they become more conscious. My professional training as a psychotherapist and Jungian analyst has included a wide-ranging study of different perspectives that have also helped me map this inner territory, revealing still more of the sources that drive all of us, for better and worse.

My search to understand what drives us has led me to some conclusions about the compulsive personality, perhaps most importantly that there is method in its "madness." I hope that sharing what I've learned will help you avoid its perils and realize its potential.

dragged along by his busy life that he would have been relieved to get the ride over with. George believed adamantly he was living the best way he could, but he didn't expect that to make him happy. He felt trapped in circumstances beyond his control.

George's parents had loved him deeply, but their anxiety spoiled most of their interactions with him. They frequently corrected him and nagged him to be more careful. The way they treated him left him feeling as if the world was a dangerous place, and that his parents felt that neither he nor they were equipped to navigate it. When other kids were riding their bikes to the mall, his parents insisted on driving him there. The humiliation was bad enough, but what was worse for him was that he felt responsible for calming his parents' anxiety. It's hard to be happy when your parents aren't secure. While many kids rebel and throw caution to the wind to deal with their overcontrolling parents, George developed a habit of trying to plan, proving to his parents that he had things under control.

Early in life he had felt a vague sense that he wanted to do big things, important things. The only book he could remember reading as a child was *The Little Engine That Could*. As early as junior high school he had felt a need to accomplish something—just what wasn't exactly clear. His college classmates liked him, but they teasingly called him Saint George, both because of his high morals (he didn't drink, smoke, or party), but also because, like his namesake medieval hero who rescued a town by slaying the poisonous dragon, it seemed that he was always on a mission.

That sense of mission found a home in architecture. Building shelter, it seemed to him, made him part of the solution, not part of the problem. It felt like the best way for him, given his particular skill set, to make a contribution to the greater good. Once George fell in love with his wife, Jenine, his interest in architecture was subsumed under what seemed to be a more pressing mission: to provide for his family. Determined but always on guard, his driven nature kicked into overdrive. He studied constantly, graduated with honors from architecture school, and eventually started his own successful firm.

George was no fun anymore. Not that he was ever the life of the party, but in the past he could at least joke, play around, and enjoy things occasionally. Even on vacation, he was usually upset because things never went exactly according to his plan, and he was always preoccupied with solving problems and planning the next hour, the next year, and the next decade.

But most of all George needed completion. A good day was when he got to check lots of tasks off his list. He couldn't tolerate anything left unresolved, and because architectural projects are long term, he was always on edge. If you got in the way of him completing a project, you'd have a very frustrated man on your hands—struggling not to be angry (because he was determined to be "good"), but seething nevertheless.

If you did get to know George better, you'd notice that he was constantly checking his watch and his phone. He always had a sense that he should be doing something else, but he'd forgotten what he originally wanted to achieve. Or, to be more philosophical, he'd forgotten what the hell he was doing on this planet at all. While he appeared to be in total control, he was really at the mercy of his demon habit—productivity. He was no longer in control of his life. Someone else was driving.

The Compulsive Urge

George is just one of millions of people who've veered into a lifestyle of compulsive doing: controlling, achieving, producing, and perfecting, well beyond any real external need. I'm describing a style of personality that affects everything they do, not just OCD, which leads to more specific intrusive thoughts and repetitive behaviors (a distinction we'll explore in chapter 1). Being compulsive can make you successful in a practical way, but it can also ruin your relationships and keep you from being fulfilled. Ironically, it can keep you from achieving other goals that would make your life satisfying and meaningful. But even when it helps you adapt well to your outer world, compulsivity often leads to a painful disaster for your inner world.

Some people who are compulsive see no problem with their way of living but are urged by family, friends, or colleagues—all bystanders who get run over by their rigid determination—to slow down and find some balance. Others have a sense that something is awry but are so addicted to their work that they can't slow down enough to see what's happening inside. Still others are forced to stop and look inside when can provide direction. This is a bottom-up, democratic approach, not a top-down, dictatorial one.

Most orthopedists will tell you that injuries often happen when you rely on one set of muscles to the exclusion of others. Certain muscles get weak and the next thing you know you're lying on the ground writhing in pain. The suffering that results from being driven by fear is similar: it develops from an unbalanced way of living in which certain psychological functions (such as willpower or delaying gratification) are developed at the expense of others (such as finding meaning or pursuing pleasure). The resulting injuries include not only actual physical ones, but also depression, burnout, anxiety, a sense of futility, and failed relationships. They may not be as obvious as a back out of whack, but they're just as painful and debilitating.

When we develop a broader sense of who we are, our steering gets better. Unhealthy compulsives try to drive willfully with a very narrow sense of their identity, and therefore with limited input on where to drive. It's the same trip over and over. In fact, it's more like being stuck on a city bus that drives the same loop every hour. When your sense of direction is informed by something greater than the conscious ego, by other aspects of your personality beyond simple willpower, the stress and anxiety that are hallmark dangers of the compulsive personality diminish.

While it might seem really strong, this determined "I," due to its inflexibility, is actually quite weak. George was identified entirely with his sense of willpower and achievement. It left him vulnerable to a crash.

We'll be checking in with George and others as we go along to see how they were able to develop a larger identity and make transitions to more fulfilling lives. The path is not easy: For reasons that are psychological, cultural, and even biochemical, changing how we live takes time, effort, and a willingness to sacrifice what seem like sacrosanct values and indispensable behaviors. It also takes a willingness to adopt new approaches that may seem threatening.

I've written this book to help you find your way back to a healthier life without taking away what is essential to you. I won't ask you to give up any of your determination—only to let go of an unbalanced insistence on one way of being so determined. I will be asking you to stretch—to consider trying and adopting ways of thinking and behaving that are different from those you've relied on. These may feel very foreign and even dangerous. I will be asking you to supplement will and intention with attitudes and behavior that include receptivity, play, and feeling. I will ask you to live not just in the future but also deeply in the present, and to value not only productivity but also process.

If you have a driven personality you know and value what it means to work hard—but this will be a very different form of hard work for you. You will need to harness your natural energy and direct it more consciously, not so much with the brute force of putting your nose to the grindstone, but rather in a more subtle way, using that energy to stop relying exclusively on productivity and perfection, and instead venturing heroically into other activities that are far less comfortable for you. It will be less like driving furiously on a straight superhighway and more like navigating the narrow winding streets of a medieval town, paying attention to things you've never noticed before.

If this seems foreign to you, consider that maybe that's a sign that you're reading exactly the right book. I'll explain what all this means in a grounded and realistic way for those of you who for whom following an inner urge seems like a detour from a more practical destination.

Who Is This Guy and Why Is He Writing This?

You may be wondering: "Does this guy get it?" "Is he compulsive?" If so, "Is he a healthy compulsive?" Yes, yes, and, for the most part, yes. Or at least I like to think so. While one reason this subject interests me is that I work with driven people every day (New York City is a magnet for driven people), another reason is that the theme of driving consciously has been at the center of much of my own life. While I believe that I've managed to spend most of my time on the healthy side of the line, I've had to work hard, ironically, not to work too hard.

In my twenty-five years of experience as a psychotherapist, I've watched people struggle with compulsivity; I've watched as people who want so much to do the right thing get pulled into the wrong thing, and I've watched as people learned how to use their energy in a more fulfilling way. Helping them has been part of my own fulfillment, and I'd like to share what I've learned with a larger audience, both those who struggle with compulsivity, and those who are affected by compulsives.

It's time that we took the stigma out of being compulsive and instead helped people to use this energy in a constructive and fulfilling way.

This has ramifications beyond the individual. It's also about the larger world that driven people affect. I venture that much of the good that's been accomplished in the world has been accomplished by people who've had compulsive tendencies. Much of the bad has been wrought by people whose intense willpower was hijacked by fear—no matter how confident they appeared to everyone around them.

The fate of our world is determined not by the people with the best ideas, but by the people with the most determination. Most of these people are driven—often to their own detriment and the detriment of others—by judgment, punishment, and unrealistic expectations. Many who end up in leadership positions are compulsive, and many of them are unhappy, unhealthy, unbalanced, and, worst of all, unconscious. We need their energy, but we should also be asking how we can help them drive better.

We can help people to be healthy compulsives—to be productive without driving themselves and everyone around them crazy. Helping them to use their energies in a conscious, balanced way is in the best interest of us all. That's the purpose of this book.

Map: How Do We Get There from Here?

I'll be citing research throughout this book to support my ideas, not to prove them. I do this with the recognition that much of the research we have is preliminary, unreplicated, and perhaps not specific to your particular situation. However, I do want to demonstrate that what I'm suggesting isn't just off the cuff and doesn't go against the scientific evidence that we do have so far.

I'll offer examples of people who've struggled with compulsivity and succeeded in finding more fulfilling ways to use their energy. These examples will be composites of people I've known personally or worked with in therapy, avoiding any possibility of identification in order to protect their privacy. For this reason these examples are not real, but they are very true. I don't want any of my clients to ever feel that their confidentiality would be compromised, or that if they "perform" well enough they would become an example for my next book. These examples are compressed and simplified for the sake of clarity. Your situation is certain to be more complex and nuanced.

Here's how we'll proceed. In Part I I'll describe the character style that I call the driven personality in more detail, differentiating the healthy and unhealthy versions of it, and distinguishing it from obsessive-compulsive disorder (OCD). I'll show how you can know where you stand on a spectrum of healthy to unhealthy. I'll also discuss what leads to a healthy or unhealthy compulsive personality. I'll outline these factors as four acts of a drama—genes, environment, coping, and maintaining—that determine where you end up on a spectrum from fulfilling to unfulfilling adjustment. Understanding the causes will be important in helping you to know why you can change and how you can change. I won't leave you a victim to either your genes or your upbringing. We'll explore an inner map of the compulsive personality, getting to know the distinct parts that sometimes take over the wheel—personifying these tendencies to make them easier to recognize.

In Part II we'll explore what it takes to help you move from the unhealthy end of the compulsive spectrum closer to the healthy end of it. We'll look first at the internal changes that need to take place—changes in how you think and how you relate to your feelings and values. Then we'll look at behavioral changes that you may need to make in your outer world.

In Part III we will apply these steps to six fulcrum issues. How you navigate these areas will determine which end of the compulsive spectrum you live on, and how fulfilling your life is.

In Part IV I'll offer suggestions for support along the way, both for compulsives and for their partners.

Let's get to work.

~

PART I

THE DRIVEN PERSONALITY: WHAT IT'S LIKE AND HOW IT GOT THAT WAY

CHAPTER ONE

Identifying the Driven Personality

People think that I am disciplined. It is not discipline. It is devotion. There is a great difference.

—Luciano Pavarotti

Let's look more closely now at the driven personality to see if it describes you or someone important to you. To do so, we'll draw on psychological theory and research, which, while most of it describes only the unhealthy end of the spectrum, will help us to understand the pattern of symptoms that often come together to create the web that traps people in compulsive behavior.

The Unhealthy End of the Spectrum: OCPD

The closest psychiatric diagnosis we have for the unhealthy version of the driven personality is obsessive-compulsive personality disorder (OCPD). I'm not crazy about using this term or any other diagnosis to label people, but the research that's been done on the condition can help us understand the people who suffer from it and help them get better. My plan is to extract what we can from what we know about OCPD without pathologizing the people whom the diagnosis is intended to help.

OCPD is different from conditions such as depression or anxiety. It's a deeply ingrained pattern that pervades the entire personality, rather than just creating specific symptoms. It usually manifests in late adolescence and causes significant suffering in relationships and functioning. As many as one out of twelve people on the street meet the criteria,[1] but most people are unaware of OCPD as a serious psychological issue, and worse, those who do have the condition don't know that they have it and that it causes their unhappiness and problems with relationships. In fact, for many this harmful condition feels like the most honorable way to approach life.

According to the American Psychiatric Association, OCPD involves "a pervasive pattern of preoccupation with orderliness, perfectionism, and mental and interpersonal control, at the expense of flexibility, openness, and efficiency, beginning by early adulthood and present in a variety of contexts."[2] If you have four or more of the following symptoms, you meet the criteria for a diagnosis of OCPD. If you have one to four of these symptoms you would be described as simply having *traits* of OCPD. These symptoms describe what can happen to someone with a driven personality when things go awry.

DSM-5 Criteria for Obsessive-Compulsive Personality Disorder

1. Is preoccupied with details, rules, lists, order, organization, or schedules to the extent that the major point of the activity is lost.
2. Shows perfectionism that interferes with task completion (e.g., is unable to complete a project because his or her own overly strict standards are not met).
3. Is excessively devoted to work and productivity to the exclusion of leisure activities and friendships (not accounted for by obvious economic necessity).
4. Is overconscientious, scrupulous, and inflexible about matters of morality, ethics, or values (not accounted for by cultural or religious identification).
5. Is unable to discard worn-out or worthless objects even when they have no sentimental value.

6. Is reluctant to delegate tasks or to work with others unless they submit to exactly his or her way of doing things.
7. Adopts a miserly spending style toward both self and others; money is viewed as something to be hoarded for future catastrophes.
8. Shows rigidity and stubbornness.

Let's check in with George to see what these look like in an actual person.

George through the Lens of OCPD

1. Clearly George was missing the point about his activities because of his preoccupation with how things were supposed to be. We know that George lost the point of vacation: rest, relaxation, and rejuvenation were eclipsed by plans and consternation. Worse, the whole point of having and providing for a family also seemed to be lost on George: while he loved them in his heart, he neglected them in his behavior. He didn't partake in the care, closeness, security, intimacy, and pleasure that one usually hopes to find in a family.
2. George was certainly perfectionistic, but he was not a procrastinator. Like many driven people, his perfectionism did not get in the way of his finishing work projects. But at the same time, those were the only projects he had; he wouldn't allow himself to try anything he wouldn't be perfect at.
3. His job did take precedence over everything else and excluded other possibilities of leisure and friendship. As often happens with people who suffer with OCPD, these symptoms got worse for George as he grew older.
4. George did maintain high moral standards. No one ever accused him of cheating. In fact, he was successful partly because of his squeaky-clean reputation. Rather, the problem was that he couldn't tolerate the idea that anyone else had ever broken a rule. If his neighbor used a leaf blower five minutes after village ordinance allowed, he'd have a fit. If his son was seven minutes late for curfew, there was hell to pay. On the road he was no saint: road rage was a real problem. He loved using his car horn

to honk at people to punish them for bad driving. He was determined to show anyone who broke the rules that he wouldn't let
them get away with it. Perhaps worse was the hell he lived inside:
not only the pressure to be good, but also the relentless judgment
of others that robbed him of any peace.

5. You should have seen George's garage. Technically he wasn't
   what we'd call a hoarder, but anything that might come in handy
   down the line was kept there: old scraps of lumber, used bicycle
   horns that no longer worked, a 1967 television set that he might
   use for parts—someday.

6. George had great difficulty delegating. While he had assistants
   on his staff, it wasn't clear who was assisting whom. He oversaw
   every detail they worked on, and it led to more than a few of
   them leaving. He just couldn't let go enough to trust that they
   would do quality work, no matter how good they were.

7. George was frugal both at work and home. On a few occasions
   his parsimony led to problems at work that ended up costing
   more money in the long run. The family budget was organized
   to the penny. Nonnecessities, much less luxury items, were not
   in the budget. This was a source of conflict with his wife, who
   knew that a home needed more than austere furniture to make
   it a home.

8. George was so stubborn that it almost cost him his marriage. He
   fought with his wife over purchasing flowers for the house, and it
   finally came down to an ultimatum from her: "George, if we can't
   buy flowers, I'm leaving you." This is when he came to see me.

More Traits Associated with Severe Compulsivity

Here are more possible downside traits that are only hinted at in the
list of criteria for OCPD:

Urgently leaning forward into the future: Unhealthy compulsives feel
an extreme urgency about their goals, large and small, and deadlines
can take on life-and-death proportions. They find it very hard to be
spontaneous and to savor the present. Patience is in short supply. Plans
trump all.

Efficiency on steroids: Most driven people hate to waste. But the un-healthy ones prioritize efficiency above other human needs. In fact, for them, efficiency is not just a priority but a reflection on character. This tendency applies to how they manage time, money, objects, and even people, and is one reason that unhealthy compulsives have difficulty throwing things out.

Rigidly idealistic: Compulsives also hold tightly to ideas. They tend to be scrupulous, but they can also become dogmatic. They may argue about details and miss the larger picture. They may hear the notes but miss the music.

A knack for obsession: Driven people may concentrate well, but they can also have difficulty moving on to another topic. Attention is sharp but limited in mobility and by a narrow range. Concentrating may become obsessing if they get stuck trying to figure out the right thing to do, especially even when there really is no black or white solution, only grey compromises.

Obligation overrides desire: "I should" replaces "I desire," often completely. Their body, beliefs, and behavior all become constricted, controlled, and censored in an effort to do what they imagine they're supposed to do. Most unhealthy compulsives have lost sight of what makes them happy and how to have fun. Instincts are lost or hijacked.

Fantasies of escape: People who suffer from OCPD and depression are more likely to attempt suicide than those with just depression. People with OCPD score lower on a test called the Reasons for Living Inventory.[3] This is what I mean when I say that they've lost track of what would truly give their lives meaning.

Human doings: Those who have succumbed to the dark side of the driven personality function as human doings rather than as human beings. Everything is measured in terms of productivity. Psychoanalyst Wilhelm Reich described compulsives as living machines.[4] Serious to a fault, most unhealthy compulsives have a high bar for humor.

Forever counting: Numbers are dangerous for compulsives: money, calories, steps walked, social media metrics (e.g., Facebook "likes"), and anything that can be measured turns into something they can become compulsive about. For some, it's all about putting points on the score-board. For others, it can lead to serious eating disorders.[5]

Fixated on fixing: Driven people tend to focus on what's wrong and needs correction. The world needs this sort of person. But the unhealthy ones will find things that are wrong—and even create them—in order to have something to fix. Further, seldom do they point out or savor what's good.

Closure or bust: Driven people need resolution and completion; it's hard for them to leave anything undone. They may love puzzles, but have a hard time leaving them behind. It's as if they have a blinding red warning light that says something is wrong until they finish a project.

If it hurts, it's good: All of these tendencies can rise to masochistic levels: they create suffering as a result of commitment to some long-forgotten goal. Some compulsives believe that if it isn't hard, it isn't really work. And of course if it isn't work, it's not only frivolous, it's totally meaningless. Suffering can become a sign of their goodness and offer certainty that they're doing the right thing.

Strengths of the Healthy Compulsive

But the symptoms of OCPD and these other characteristics of unhealthy compulsives describe only the negative development of characteristics of the driven personality, characteristics that could otherwise be extremely beneficial. The driven person may be steadfast rather than stiff, organized rather than controlling, determined rather than severe, independent rather than obstinate, and trustworthy rather than moralistic.[6]

Let's review the "symptoms" of OCPD to see what they would look like if these tendencies were developed in a beneficial way. In this case healthy compulsives:

1. Are capable of intense focus and concentration that helps them to be meticulous, punctual, reliable, organized, and able to delay gratification in order to complete tasks.
2. Have high standards for the quality of their work.
3. Are conscientiousness and committed to their work and relationships.
4. Maintain high moral values.
5. Are very efficient and not wasteful.
6. Are able to work independently to bring projects to conclusion.

7. Are thrifty and conscious about their spending; they manage money to the advantage of themselves and those around them.
8. Have strength, determination, and a keen sense of time that help them to maintain quality despite difficult circumstances.

Certainly this is a list of desirable characteristics for any partner or worker, be it a tailor who makes perfect alterations at a reasonable price or an auto mechanic whom you can trust to keep your car running well. Notice how the same personality tendencies can lead to very different outcomes. The healthy compulsive, by maintaining awareness and prioritizing values, can use this predisposition in a way that's not counterproductive.[7]

Distinguishing Compulsive Personality from Obsessive-Compulsive Disorder

Orcadia

George's office manager, Orcadia, had a different form of compulsivity than he did. Her anxiety led her to engage in repetitive rituals, like locking the door at her home three times before leaving. She might also have to go back inside to make sure the iron was off. She'd get strange, disturbing, and intrusive ideas that she'd fight off by wearing certain colors. For instance, when her cousin James had to go to the doctor, she couldn't stop worrying that something terrible was going to happen to him if she didn't wear her blue blouse. She'd get very anxious if you didn't take off your shoes when you walked into her house, and she liked to have everything arranged at fixed right angles.

But unlike George, Orcadia had no trouble leaving work right at five and going home to her family, where she'd joke with them, watch television, and relax. When she went on vacation, her favorite thing to do was sit by the pool and read crime novels. Her desk was always perfectly neat, and she wasn't defensive about it. When anyone teased her about a clear desk being a sign of a sick mind, she laughed it off. She didn't have rigid ideas about how people should behave that would leave her feeling a need to appear virtuous. She'd be happy to get rid of her anxiety and quirks, but she was not gripped by the need to work, produce, or complete. She was not driven.

Orcadia serves as a good example of someone with obsessive compulsive disorder (OCD), in contrast to George, who had obsessive-compulsive *personality* disorder (OCPD). The fact that you're compulsive or driven doesn't mean that you have OCD, which is a whole 'nother kettle of symptoms from OCPD. There is some overlap between them,[8] but they're actually two distinct patterns. The similar terminology is very unfortunate; it often confuses people rather than helps them understand and diminish their suffering.

The effects of OCD range from mildly annoying to entirely debilitating. People with OCD tend to engage in rituals and checking, need to have things in order, fear contamination, and tend to hoard. In order to avoid disturbing obsessions, they engage in repetitive behavior, such as washing their hands fifty times a day, locking the door five times before they leave, and repeatedly checking the oven to make sure that it's off. Unlike George and most people with OCPD, Orcadia was not in the habit of delaying rewards[9]—she didn't have to finish a project before she let herself have a margarita. Or three.

OCPD permeates the entire personality, whereas while OCD makes people anxious, it doesn't infect their entire personality. People with OCPD tend to be more domineering, while people with OCD tend to be more submissive because of their anxiety.[10] Until they crash or are confronted, people like George and others with OCPD usually feel that their lifestyle makes total sense. Orcadia and others who suffer from OCD don't want to have their obsessive thoughts or rituals.

People with OCD often begin to experience their symptoms in early childhood while people with OCPD start to see them in their late teens or early twenties. There seem to be stronger biological and genetic origins for OCD than for OCPD, which would explain why OCD responds more to medication than OCPD does.

I should also clarify the difference between obsessions and compulsions: obsessions refers to intrusive or repetitive thoughts, whereas compulsions refer to driven, repetitive, or ritualistic behavior. People who are obsessive often engage in compulsions to try to get rid of their obsessions. They may have trouble making decisions, which may lead them to procrastinate rather than complete or even begin projects. While these obsessive traits and procrastination may be associated with compulsions, they don't always lead to compulsive behavior.

Another important distinction to make when trying to understand compulsivity is that some people develop addictions that might be described as compulsive, such as addictions to sex, gambling, shopping, or an endless search for the perfect caramel flan. These very specific compulsions usually don't emerge from the foundation of a driven personality. While they can destroy your life, they don't infect the entire personality with the same pattern of symptoms. However, in rare cases someone who's driven may funnel all of their passion into one particular compulsion.

Self-Test

If you're curious whether you meet the criteria for OCPD, here's a self-test to give you a rough sense of where you stand. While it's not really possible to give yourself a medical diagnosis from a test such as this, it can be helpful to get a relative sense of how severe your symptoms are. If you can, have someone who knows you well go through the questions with you. They might see you differently from the way you see yourself—and that could be enlightening.

Leonard Cammer's OCPD Self-Test[11]
Answer each statement below on a scale of 1 to 4:
>   1 = None or a little of the time
>   2 = Some of the time
>   3 = Good part of the time
>   4 = Most or all of the time

1. I prefer things to be done my way.
2. I am critical of people who don't live up to my standards or expectations.
3. I stick to my principles, no matter what.
4. I am upset by changes in the environment or the behavior of people.
5. I am meticulous and fussy about my possessions.
6. I get upset if I don't finish a task.
7. I insist on full value for everything I purchase.
8. I like everything I do to be perfect.
9. I follow an exact routine for everyday tasks.
10. I do things precisely to the last detail.

11. I get tense when my day's schedule is upset.
12. I plan my time so that I won't be late.
13. It bothers me when my surroundings are not clean and tidy.
14. I make lists for my activities.
15. I think that I worry about minor aches and pains.
16. I like to be prepared for any emergency.
17. I am strict about fulfilling every one of my obligations.
18. I think that I expect worthy moral standards in others.
19. I am badly shaken when someone takes advantage of me.
20. I get upset when people do not replace things exactly as I left them.
21. I keep used or old things because they might still be useful.
22. I think that I am sexually inhibited.
23. I find myself working rather than relaxing.
24. I prefer being a private person.
25. I like to budget myself carefully and live on a cash and carry basis.

Total your answers to get your score. Typically, people score between 50 and 75. But anywhere above 70 means you're on the unhealthy end of the spectrum.

- 25–45 = not uptight;
- 46–55 = usefully compulsive;
- 56–70 = moderately compulsive;
- above 70, danger zone!

Whatever your score on this test, the real question is whether the tendencies you do have are so dominant that they exclude other aspects of your life that would help you to be more balanced and fulfilled. (Or, if you live or work with someone who is compulsive, whether you find yourself having to constrict to accommodate them.)

If it does seem that you've been driven into some unhealthy compulsive territory, you may be wondering, "What can I do about it? How can I find my way back to a more satisfying way of living?" We'll get there, but first we'll need to slow down, backtrack, and see how you got here in the first place. This will be essential in helping you to get your bearings, and in understanding what you'll need to do to get back on track to a more fulfilling and balanced life.

CHAPTER TWO

~

How Did I Get This Way?
The Tree Grows Where It Can

We first make our habits, then our habits make us.

—John Dryden

Adapt or perish, now as ever, is Nature's inexcusable imperative.

—H. G. Wells

I was persisting in reading my present environment in the light of my old one.

—Richard Wright, *Black Boy*

Sharon

To say Sharon taught violin would be like saying Michael Jordan played basketball. She was deeply invested in her students' success and she was a star at facilitating it. She'd studied with the best and knew what it took to make it in the classical concert world.

At first glance you might think she was deriving vicarious and narcissistic gratification from her students' achievements—that she loved the glory that came with them winning competitions and getting into the best conservatories. While that certainly was part of the reward for her, something more fundamental drove her: she needed to do things the "right" way. She knew how Bach and Mozart were supposed to be played, and she felt she had to pass it on. Playing them any other way was just indulgent, and she wasn't going to let that happen to any student who came under her tutelage.

Sharon demanded a great deal from her students and herself. She always went the extra mile to help—attending all their concerts, strategizing with their parents, and getting their recommendations in on time. As a mentor she encouraged her students to take responsibility and to carry themselves with dignity and respect. While stoic, she also cared deeply. For some students, Sharon's direction was immensely helpful for their careers and maturity. They came out the other side of training with self-esteem and with appreciation for her commitment.

But for other students, her approach was poison, neither professionally nor personally helpful. These students left hurt and confused about themselves and the music they had once loved. Sharon tried to shut these out of her mind and justify her rigorous approach. If they didn't have the discipline for music, it was best they find out sooner rather than later. But she wasn't entirely convinced, and she sometimes wondered about the emotional price her students had to pay to earn the attention she offered.

If her devotion to teaching was the only place she was compulsive, we might just chalk it up to pedagogical philosophy and let it go. But Sharon's insistence on doing everything the right way affected her entire personality, from her healthy diet, to the cultured decorations in her apartment, to how quickly she rejected potential partners who weren't up to standard—which meant all of them. Like a virus, perfectionism was taking over her life.

It was striking and sad that a woman who had been so alive and so intensely moved by music early in her life was slowly dying of emotional thirst. She was only forty-four, but she already seemed worn down by life; she seldom experienced joy. While she still took pride in her successful students, she began to notice that she wasn't fulfilled by seeing them do well.

She'd been a very promising violinist herself when she was younger, but her own career as a performer had slowly come to an end in her twenties. Her passion and talent for music as a child had been hijacked by a need to impress others. Her alcoholic father and status-conscious mother had divorced when she was eleven, leaving her feeling responsible to rescue the family reputation. Over time she became so perfectionistic that she also became too nervous to perform.

While Sharon still had some friends from her training, she was no longer close to them. She could be judgmental of others, and her schoolmarm righteousness turned people off. She taught at a high school for the arts that prepared students to enter prestigious conservatories. She was immensely respected, but regarded with trepidation by students, faculty, and administration. Because she saw so many students, she had little time or energy left for socializing anyway.

Eventually something happened that made her pause and question how she was living. One of her students, one who tried desperately to please Sharon, broke down crying during her lesson. This wasn't exactly the first time a student had cried in her lesson, but this was different. This student was going through family problems like the ones Sharon had experienced, and it brought her back to her own childhood. She recalled a day when she had cried in her own lesson. She had felt so humiliated that she swore she would never let herself be so vulnerable again. After her student left, Sharon broke down crying herself for the first time in decades; despondent that not only had she lost the real passion she had had for music as a child, but also that she was still living as she had when she was twelve years old, trying to prove that she was acceptable.

Sharon serves as a good example of someone who had been driven early in life and became rigidly compulsive as she grew older. Like many people who want to change their lives, to move forward she needed to backtrack to see where she'd made a wrong turn. Looking back on our history need not get us stuck in the past. In fact, reflecting on what's happened can actually keep us from living in the past—from living as if we still need to fix what had needed fixing in the past.

The Four-Act Play of Personality Development

To understand how you've gotten to where you are, let's look at personality development as a four-act play in which the driven personality evolves into one that is somewhere on a spectrum between healthy and unhealthy.

Act 1: Nature

In Act 1 you're born with a particular genetic predisposition for a given temperament, the seed that contains the rough plan for the tree. This is "nature," your constitution that results from heredity. Ask most parents about their kids, and they'll tell you that they sensed right away that their child came, to some extent, prepackaged with his or her own personality—before there was any chance for parental imprinting. It would be misleading to say that nature intentionally makes us different, as if it had a grand plan to create specialists. But those species that do have individuals with differing individual capacities have survived and thrived because they could adapt to a wider range of circumstances. With their unique capacities, people who are driven have played an important role in our evolution.

We have scientific support for a genetic foundation of the compulsive personality from two sources: studies of identical twins who were raised apart, and neurobiological research that uses scans to study the brains of people with OCPD.[1] Based on the twin studies, it seems that anywhere from 27 percent to 78 percent of the traits of compulsivity are inherited.[2] Pinning down specifically what the inherited aspects of the driven personality are is a very complicated matter; it's not the result of one specific gene. Rather it seems to be the result of a collection of genes that are expressed to varying degrees.

Here are some character traits that research indicates are at least partially inborn:

- A capacity to imagine the future, predict, control, plan, and engage in goal-directed behavior[3]
- A greater than normal capacity to perceive details[4]
- A tendency to be pressured, hard-driving, and ambitious[5]
- A tendency to be perfectionistic[6]
- A capacity for self-restraint[7]
- A capacity for grit, determination, and perseverance[8]
- A motivation to master skills and problems[9]
- An usually large emphasis on seeking behavior: learning, accomplishing, and achieving[10]
- An inclination for self-determined behavior[11]
- A capacity for intense concentration or flow[12]

- Conscientiousness[13]
- Prudence (including frugality, cautiousness, carefulness, discretion, moderation, and being prepared)[14]
- Moral indignation: criticizing others for laziness or stinginess[15]

These genes serve a purpose. Nature is happy to have some of us evolve with a compulsive style to improve our chances of surviving and spreading our genes. Thinking ahead and being careful have kept us alive—though rather anxious. Nature doesn't care if these genes drive us crazy. Like it or not, being driven has helped humans to endure, so those genes have been passed down.

This doesn't mean that you'll be just like your parents. Your parents may have passed along recessive genes, genes that they carried but weren't expressed or activated in them. Genes may also spontaneously alter, creating variations that make you different from your parents.

Let's see how the driven personality manifested in the childhoods of our examples:

Early on George proved to be a determined and perfectionistic planner who paid attention to detail. His family and teachers noticed that he not only liked to build with blocks, but that he was also intensely determined to build the best castle ever. He would be very careful to make sure the blocks were evenly balanced so that the whole thing wouldn't fall down. He'd get upset if you interrupted him. He was an indomitable little tyke.

Sharon responded to music with fascination from the time she was in the crib. She listened intently when her mother played recordings. As she grew, she began to sing constantly. She was by nature meticulous. Unlike most children, she didn't need to be goaded to practice. She sawed away at her "Twinkle-Twinkle" variation endlessly in her room. She was energetic and exuberant, but at the same time she could contain and direct her enthusiasm.

But as is the case for anyone with a driven personality, George and Sharon had far more to their constitutions than determination and perfection. Even if you were born with compulsive genes, that's only part of your makeup. You've got lots of other aspects of your personality that also crave expression. Whether there is a battle for dominance between these parts or cooperation among them will be played out in the next three acts.

Act 2: Nurture—Family and Environment
In Act 2 you're born into a particular environment: the soil, air, climate, and space where the seed comes to rest. This is "nurture," the parenting and culture you're exposed to that shapes the genes you were born with. This environment may lead you to feel secure and safe to be yourself and develop your gifts. Or it could lead you to feel insecure and vulnerable to abandonment, criticism, or punishment. Being completely authentic, which includes not only your driven qualities but also your emotions and more spontaneous behavior, might feel dangerous.

There are many scenarios that can lead to a child feeling insecure. Even if your parents tried their best to do what they believed was the "right" thing, they may have failed to tailor their rules to your particular personality. Here are some situations that may have led you to feel insecure. Notice if any of them resonate with your experience.

1. You experienced your parents as rigid and critical, or shaming of behavior that was messy or playful. If there was love or affection, it felt conditional, based on compliance: how "well" you behaved or how much you achieved.[16]
2. It seemed that your parents disapproved of any strong feelings you might have had, including anger, sadness, fear, or exuberance.
3. You experienced your parents as intrusive. They may have been so affectionate, hovering, or smothering that you feared losing yourself in enmeshed relationships. Your need for privacy and independence was not recognized.
4. Your household felt chronically chaotic, or things may have gone wrong such as disasters, health troubles, or financial problems, leaving you feeling powerless and helpless.
5. You perceived your parents' overprotectiveness as an indication that the world is a dangerous place.[17]
6. You experienced your parents as anxious and needy. This could have been because their insecurity was extreme, or because you were especially sensitive to their condition. In either case you felt you needed to attend to their needs to the exclusion of your own.[18]
7. Your early relationships felt disappointing, and you felt that you couldn't depend on others for security.

8. Your parents did not provide clear standards, leaving you to develop them for yourself before you were ready to.
9. Your parents and culture emphasized looks over feeling. They emphasized "What will people think if you wear that skirt?" rather than "Are you comfortable in that?"

George's Act 2 shows a family high on protection and low on interaction. They tried to make sure that things were safe in the house and that he didn't get hurt or get sick. But there wasn't much affection. George got a strong sense of who he was *supposed* to be, but no sense of who he *really* was. His enthusiastic efforts to build, create, and learn were met not with pleasure or encouragement, but with warnings that he had better get things right or things would go wrong. They didn't give him any reason to feel good about himself.

Sharon's Act 2 includes a father whose drinking made him belligerent and unpredictable and a mother who needed desperately to impress others. They paid little attention to her unless she was doing something they thought precocious. She felt inadequate and loved only conditionally, only when she was achieving something that looked impressive. She felt ashamed of her family's situation and herself.

Whatever your parents and environment were like, one of the most influential factors in your development was whether you had a sense of security in your relationships, and a sense that it was safe being yourself in those relationships. Even rigid and overprotective parenting doesn't necessarily turn you into an unhealthy compulsive—if your parents forge strong relationships with you. Children who don't form secure attachments with their caregivers, and so don't feel that they can be themselves, are more likely to suffer from OCPD.[19] If you have controlling parents, but you also have a strong connection with them, you are less likely to develop OCPD.

Notice that I speak of your *experience* of your parents, not historical facts. We'll never know exactly what they were like as parents, and children don't always perceive or remember their parents accurately. Yet still, your experience of your parents is very real—wonderful or painful—and that has played a role in the development of your personality. Further, whenever something in the present resembles difficult issues from your past, you may feel as if you are right back in the difficult situation from the past—even if the trigger is relatively small.

In addition to the influence of family, we need to consider how our larger environment shapes us: peers, school, community, and culture. Any of these aspects of our environment may either force hyperdevelopment of compulsive tendencies or discourage any appropriate cultivation of them.

Peer groups exert a great deal of power during adolescence and often use shaming, exclusion, and bullying as negative incentives to conform. Energy that might have gone into learning might get funneled into appearance. Local communities may feel so closed-minded to us that we dissent and isolate, and we have no place to use our energy. For better and worse, culture has a parental aspect; it imposes society's rules and plays a major role in the development of a compulsive style. Beginning in grade school and ending only with death, most developed economies reward compulsive behavior, not spontaneity. As with parents, your culture may leave you feeling that it's not safe to be authentic, and a conflict ensues about whether it's best to comply, or to be true to yourself.[20] One of the things that makes OCPD difficult to treat is that it must be the most culturally sanctioned psychological disorder in history: it's rewarded with promotions, status, and money.

The question then becomes: how did you cope with this conflict? Not everyone responds in the same way to the same environment. This leads us to our third act.

Act 3: The Child Develops a Coping Strategy

In Act 3, before you were old enough to realize what you were doing, you began to develop a strategy that helped you to cope with the fit between your predisposition and your environment. Those with a good fit and a secure environment could follow their passions out of desire rather than fear. But many driven people who were born into an environment where they felt insecure had to use their energy and talent to try to feel more secure. To the degree that they needed to do this, they became healthy or unhealthy compulsives.[21]

To return to the seed and tree analogy, seeds find a way to become trees, using their DNA to get exposure to the sun's rays and to grow, even if that means growing in a crooked fashion, growing toward the side, rather than straight up toward the sky. Children will find a way to grow and survive psychologically, bending and twisting their personality however they need to in order to adapt to their situation.

We all develop our own coping strategies: different children respond differently to similar situations. We could look back to your childhood, find a punishing parent and say "*Aha!* That's why you're compulsive." People often say, "I got that from my mother" or "That's because of my father." It's not so simple. This is a common and misleading conception of human development. There is no one-to-one correlation between how parents treat their children and how they develop. We also need to consider the nature of the child who was born to those parents. The interaction between those two will determine how they learn to adapt.

Some research supports the idea that punishing parents are likely to raise compulsive children, yet not all children respond to punishment by becoming compulsive. Others become desperately dependent, devotedly rebellious, or passively noncompliant. So, we can't simply identify something about your parents or your environment as the sole cause of your personality.

We need to ask empathically, what did you do to cope with your environment when you began to feel insecure or conflicted? Even though it was chosen unconsciously, and partly because it was chosen unconsciously, that approach to coping affected—and still affects—your personality. Did you start excluding some parts of your personality and emphasizing others? Did you become a good boy or girl, relying on your capacity to plan ahead to protect you from getting in trouble or being abandoned? Did you compensate for a fear of getting out of control by being very controlling? Did you become determined to be the most impressive student in the school?[22]

To the extent that you felt secure, you began to use your talents in a healthy way that left you well-adjusted and fulfilled. You helped edit the paper at school but then goofed off with your friends before going home to do a reasonable amount of studying. To the extent that you felt insecure and that you needed to make sure you weren't criticized or abandoned, you may have begun to use your exacting energy in defensive and unhealthy ways, being perfectionist and overworking, for instance, to avoid being judged, feeling guilty, or getting "out of control."

You edited the school paper and yearbook and then went home and spent the entire evening studying so that your parents wouldn't accuse you of slacking off.

Recall the studies I noted that indicated that some people with OCPD were raised in families where they didn't develop secure relationships. It would make sense that those who were born with a driven personality and didn't feel secure in their relationships would use their talents to compensate for the feelings that they were unworthy or unloved. When all you've got is a hammer, everything looks like a nail. The hammer wasn't really the only tool they had, but perfectionism and productivity certainly seemed the easiest ones to use at the time.

This situation leads to a painful negative feedback loop: insecure children use their natural energy and diligence to give their parents and culture what they seem to want from them, and then the child resents having to be so good. Their resentment leads them to feel more insecure because they aren't supposed to be angry. Then they try to compensate for their transgression with more compliance, which leads to more angry resentment, and so on.

Let's review the list of scenarios from Act 2 to see some typical coping strategies driven kids adopt to feel more secure:

Parents critical of behavior. If you experienced your parents as critical of behavior that was messy or impulsive, you may have enlisted your capacity for self-restraint, planning, and perfectionism, and excluded the more playful and spontaneous parts of yourself to avoid feeling rejected by your parents. Staying out of trouble became your goal. You became a devoted altar boy, high-achieving girl scout, or unbeatable swimmer to prove your goodness.

Parents critical of feelings. If you experienced your parents as critical of your feelings, and you felt that your feelings put you at risk of criticism or abandonment, you may have used your capacity for self-restraint to gain control of all your emotional states so they didn't endanger you. You were the teacher's pet and everyone said what a good kid you were. All your feelings went into your journal and stayed there. Eventually you forgot you had feelings.

Chaotic home. If your household felt chaotic when you were a child, you may have used your capacity to plan and bring order to your life, both your feelings and your environment, by organizing, making lists, and planning. No one ever had to tell you to do your homework. You had the best baseball card collection in the neighborhood. You saved every penny you made mowing lawns.

Overprotective parents. If you perceived your parents' overprotectiveness as an indication that the world was a dangerous place, you may have relied on your capacity for self-restraint, becoming especially careful, distrusting your feelings, and delaying gratification, to make sure that you didn't put yourself in harm's way. You volunteered for the school safety patrol and your favorite thing to do was play with the family first aid kit—packing and unpacking it several times each week. Or you started working out at the gym and sought a reputation as the strongest kid on campus. Some kids called you bossy. Some may have felt you were a bully.

Anxious parents. If you felt that your parents were anxious and needy, you may have enlisted your organizing capacities to make them feel safe, but ignored your own needs to do so. You never complained. You obsessed long and hard about choosing perfect birthday gifts.

Disappointing relationships. If your early relationships felt disappointing, and you felt that getting close to someone would inevitably lead to suffering, you may have concluded that you weren't worthy, and then developed your capacity to focus on work as a substitute for intimacy. Your grades were perfect. You became a long-distance runner.

Lack of stability. If there were problems in your home such as financial crises, natural disasters, or health problems and you felt vulnerable, you may have taken responsibility for situations that were not in your control in order to feel as if things were controllable. You cooked breakfast. You planned to become an accountant.

No parental standards. If your parents didn't provide clear standards, you may have developed them on your own, and developed ones that were unrealistically high. You were the captain of the track team and all you could think about was breaking school records. Your moral development was way ahead of schedule. You pointed out your parents' hypocrisies, such as lambasting marijuana and then driving tipsy.

Emphasis on appearance. If your parents emphasized how you looked rather than how you felt, you may have become fastidious about your appearance with the hope that you wouldn't be shamed by others outside of the family. You scoured every fashion magazine you could get your hands on to figure out how you were supposed to dress. You became very competitive and set your sights on being named "Best Dressed" in the high school yearbook.

None of these strategies necessarily sound the death knell for the soul of the child. In fact, in some cases these situations allow the child to begin to develop skills and resilience in a way that will serve him or her well. But to the degree that these strategies became rigid and exclude other parts of the personality, the individual is more likely to become unhealthily compulsive.

As with all of us, George was too young during his third act to be aware how he was dealing with his family. While he loved building models, he also needed love from others. His family seemed to express love only by ensuring safety, and this didn't meet George's needs. He began to unconsciously calculate how he could get love. "So," he surmised, "if I work really hard to build the blocks so they won't fall, or get good grades, or dress just right, maybe they'll stop correcting me and instead they'll say something nice or give me a hug." He developed a strategy that enlisted his skills to fit in with his family's overly cautious approach to life. He no longer built because he wanted to. He built because he *needed* to—and that changed everything.

In Sharon's third act she became determined to be successful to help her mother and herself feel better. She studied hard in school and never misbehaved. She had always loved playing music, but as she grew older it became the platform to prove she was at least respectable. For Sharon and most compulsives, this extra effort is caused not by a narcissistic need to feel better than everyone else, but rather by a fear of not even being acceptable, not up to standard, based on a very high bar and a narrow sense of what's important.

Long-term, deep change will require that you understand why you adopted your compulsive strategy so that you can make more conscious choices about how to best use your skills and passions. Your basic personality will not change dramatically, but how it's expressed can change significantly—if you're willing to question your strategy for handling fears. This leads us to the fourth act.

Act 4: Maintenance of a Compulsive Style
In Act 4 of the evolution of your personality, as an adult you either *continue* to use the child's adaptive strategy in a way that perpetuates

it, or you develop new ones. The tree either continues to grow to the side, or, if the blocks to the sunlight are removed, the tree can grow more directly toward the sky.

If as a child you felt secure and developed healthy strategies, in your fourth act you can continue to use your exacting energy in advantageous ways, benefiting yourself and those around you. On the other hand, if as a child you tried to excel as a way to compensate for your fears, you may advance to becoming a confirmed workaholic as an adult.

But if you don't continue to invest in the old and less healthy compulsive strategy, the pattern will eventually fade. You can live out of desire and passion rather than fear and need. If you don't feed the beast, it dies off. You don't slay it—you starve it. Thus the importance of the fourth act in this play.

More so than those of most other personality disorders, the symptoms of OCPD can diminish over time—if they get deliberate attention, either on your own or with professional help. But if we continue to use unhealthy strategies, the symptoms tend to get worse.[23] Compulsive living is progressive: if you continue to rely on it as you get older, you'll only become grumpier and more persnickety—not to mention seriously depressed.[24] While folks with OCPD can change and become healthier, the symptoms don't go away accidentally.

In order to remain anxious, you have to keep avoiding the feelings and situations that make you anxious. If the anxiety-provoking situation is faced rather than avoided, it becomes less anxiety provoking. Avoidance reinforces anxiety. Psychologist George Weinberg says that compulsions persist because the person unknowingly reinforces them in the same form year after year.[25]

Avoidance of the feeling or situation we dread reinforces and sustains our anxiety partly because it increases the need that it tries to satisfy. If you try to improve self-esteem through achievement, you feed the idea that you need to prove your worth, rather than investing in the belief that you're basically good, whether you scale Mount Everest or not. If your strategy is to feel better through achievement, the need to succeed becomes insatiable because it only reinforces a sense of unworthiness. Compulsive succeeding reinforces a sense of low self-esteem because you really aren't facing the thing you fear the most. For some people, part of the problem is that they've been so good at succeeding they've never accepted themselves without the merit badges to prove their worth.

Along with what I'm describing as a psychological process, there is an underlying, parallel biological process that makes compulsive behavior an addictive habit. Research is making clear that it's possible to become addicted not only to substances, but also to behaviors.[26] Any behavior that is repeated for psychological reasons may begin to change the way your neurochemical reward system works. You may begin to need to do more and more of the behavior to get the chemical rewards it gave you at first. This seems to be the case with work and productivity.

Ever notice how good you feel when you complete a project? You're probably getting a very sweet hit of endorphins, naturally occurring pleasure hormones. A particular part of your brain becomes activated, and boy does it feel good.

Endorphins are morphine-like chemicals that the body produces to diminish pain and stimulate positive feelings. So, if you feel anxious, you get some work done, and presto, you feel better because of the endorphin fix you get when you cross something off your list. Rinse and repeat and you've got yourself an addiction.

To make matters worse, once your endorphin hit wears off, you quickly feel empty and in need of another hit. You'd expect that this would just make you want to complete another project. While that's true, it's a little more complicated—and more addictive.

When you start to worry about the new round of projects, you get a blast of another hormone, the stress hormone cortisol. This new stage of worrying and its patron hormone has its own biological payoff: increased energy. Cortisol puts your system on high alert and promotes a sense of elevated danger—a good thing if a tiger is coming after you, not a good thing just because your kitchen isn't spotless. While cortisol is associated with stress, it also serves as a reward mechanism: but the reward is energy, not pleasure. However, you could still become addicted to stress and cortisol because of the energy it provides: nature's incentive for being compulsive.[27]

In his fourth act, George has grown up, and while the outer circumstances of his life are different, he's still using the same strategies to cope with his anxiety. "If I work until 3:00 a.m., I can get this project ready so that my clients won't be upset with me. Maybe they'll say it's a great design. But at least they'll see that I've worked hard on it." He maintained his compulsive tendencies rather than facing the feelings that he was trying to avoid—unworthy and vulnerable to rejection. He displaced his anxiety onto his work. Each project was a danger to be mastered, a problem to be solved. By focusing on the external situation, he was able to avoid the inner situation. But the inner one only got worse that way, leading to a more desperate sense of need. Until he decided to change, he continued to feed his real dragon—an addiction to work—rather than starve it.

In her fourth act, Sharon switched from performing to teaching, but she was still trying to use music to feel good about herself. Trying harder and harder to be "good" by being "right," she became more rigid as she grew older. Because this strategy never really got to the root of her issue, she continued to feel that she was lovable only insofar as she achieved, and a painful cycle ensued.

With an understanding of how you became compulsive—the interplay of your genes, environment, strategy, and continued use of that strategy—you can shift how you handle your fears. You can begin to respond to your passions in more satisfying ways that lead to healthier and sustainable outcomes. It's not simple or easy, but one good thing about being driven is that you have the inner resources and determination necessary for change.

PART II

~

REALIZING YOUR DRIVEN POTENTIAL

CHAPTER THREE

Four Steps to Becoming
a Healthier Compulsive

Everyone thinks of changing the world, but no one thinks of changing himself.

—Leo Tolstoy

Becoming a healthier compulsive is not easy. It requires commitment and a willingness to change your priorities. But there is wisdom and guidance that can help make the path clearer so that you can use your energy effectively. I've condensed what I've learned from my professional and personal experience, and what we know from research,[1] into four main steps:

1. Insight: Identify your story, the inner characters in that story, and the strategy you developed for dealing with that story.
2. Emotion: Engage emotionally with deeper layers of feeling and parts of yourself.
3. Meaning: Set priorities and aspirations based on your values.
4. Action: Commit to behavior that honors your aspirations.

Let's break this down a bit more:

1. To achieve insight, you'll need to identify the story you've told yourself about life, the parts of you that have engaged in that

drama, and the strategy you developed to deal with that story. Then you'll need to question that story. For instance: Do you really need to be a policeman to the entire world to feel like a decent person? Or be the perfect parent to be loved?

2. To actually change, you'll need to allow yourself to have a richer emotional experience. We do this by allowing ourselves to feel the feelings we've avoided by working, and to feel deeper levels of emotion that may be covered over. It also involves forging a connection with the different parts of our personality, including the ones that are too dominant and the ones that have been ignored, and empathically understanding why they feel they need to do what they do. Why has that very loud and bossy voice inside of your head constantly told you to get things done and done right? Why has the more fun-loving or reflective part had to go into hiding? This step cannot be just intellectual: it needs to be experiential.

3. Once you understand your story and strategy, and you've begun to develop better emotional connections within, you will need to establish aspirations and priorities that have meaning for you. Determine where your drives, urges, and compulsions really want to go rather than just how to stay safe or out of trouble. For instance, what is it that you had hoped to gain with success? Is there a better way to achieve that?

4. Then choose actions that honor your aspirations. Develop intentions to behave differently and stick with them—even when you have setbacks. For instance, you may choose to commit to making fewer critical comments, spending more time with friends or family, or taking weekly or daily time to practice relaxing in order to break an addiction to productivity and to form better relationships.

While at first some of these suggestions might seem simplistic and others impossible, know that over time they will each build on the others and work together successfully. These steps tend to happen in the order I've presented them for most people, but the distinctions aren't clear. You will probably have emotional experiences while outlining your story, and your emotional experiences will also help you to see your story and strategy. Both will lend themselves to clarifying what has the most meaning to you. You may choose to do the first three steps in a different order. However, the temptation for some is to gloss over the inner work of insight, emotion, and meaning, and jump right in to action, doing the outer work. That's part of the problem. Without the foundation of the inner work, the outer work will not be as effective.

As an example of how to make change, I'll tell you Frank's story. We'll follow him through all of these steps to see what he did to become a healthier compulsive.

Frank: A Bully for The Good

"I didn't mean to knock over the coffeepot. I just pushed a little too hard." Frank was trying to explain to his captain how the large metal coffee urn in the police headquarters kitchen had sailed over the counter, across the room, and into the wall, where it came to an early demise. His captain still thought he'd better get some help. Anger management. Frank decided it was better to go voluntarily rather than be forced into it. So he told his captain he'd go. He told himself he wouldn't go soft.

Five feet eleven, stocky, with very short hair and a thick five o'clock shadow already at 11:00 in the morning, Frank struck me as a bear that had had too much caffeine. As we spoke, I could sense his restless energy: feet up off the floor and back down, arms twisting all around, torso and head leaning forward. He didn't know quite what to do with himself.

He told me he was forty-three and worked as a detective in a small force in a quiet midsize suburban town. Nothing exciting, but they still needed somebody to do investigations. When the only other detective on the force retired, they didn't hire a second one because they knew Frank would do the work of two—if not three or four. Frank was proud of this, and it was clear that whether the work was exciting or not, he was committed to it, and he took it very seriously. "People tell me I'm really intense. Maybe so. I have a cow when people get sloppy or lazy. It doesn't matter if we lose the case or not. It's the idea of it. I try not to lose my temper but sometimes I get a little out of control. I guess I'm a bit of a bully. But I'm a bully for The Good."

Once we got to the incident with the coffeepot, Frank wanted to minimize it. That day he'd been furious because the city was cutting back on personal days in the latest contract negotiations. It just wasn't right. Again, it was the idea of it. Everybody knew that Frank almost never took sick days, much less personal days. They'd all signed on to the force with certain expectations, and the city wasn't honoring them. Frank always did what he said he'd do, and he always said what he would do. He expected everyone else to do the same. But no matter how much he fought the reduced benefits package as the union rep, the administration wouldn't back down. The issue was out of his control and that sent him out of control. The injustice of it only added fuel to his fire.

But it didn't take much exploration to see that it wasn't just this one situation that was at issue; this was the pattern of his personality.

His girlfriend of five years was also familiar with his "intensity." "I know that she loves me. Somehow she's gotten this idea that I'm really a good guy underneath it all. But she also says I'm really stubborn and that I have rigid expectations of people. Why is it unrealistic to expect people to show up on time? It drives me crazy when she's late." He acknowledged that he overreacted at times, and he tried not to get caught up in setting her straight, but too often he just couldn't let her get away with it. He was always in policeman mode.

Frank told me that he'd been raised in a strict Italian American Roman Catholic family. His father was authoritarian, and his mother was submissive. With his father working at night, and his mother depressed, Frank was responsible for keeping an eye on his younger brothers and sister. He protected them, but he also kept them in line. He didn't tolerate misbehavior. He also paid lots of attention to fairness. Who got how much of what was a matter of great concern to him.

He had a peculiar interest in time and timing. He measured time in minutes and seconds, not days or even hours. He hadn't cared too much about school; it seemed a waste of time to him, and he hated to waste time. His real passion was baseball. He watched it on television and memorized team and player statistics inside out. He made varsity his freshman year and was captain of the team by his junior year. Ditto in college. It was the only thing that kept him in school. His talent for timing was part of what made him a great baseball player. It helped him bat, catch, throw, and steal bases—his only vice.

He had had no direction in college, but two of his uncles were police officers and he thought that might be a good career for him. Once he was on the force, his attention to detail and his dogged determination for justice landed him in the detective department. Nothing got past him. If you were guilty, you didn't want him on your case; but if you were innocent, you could count on fair treatment.

It was nearing the end of our initial consultation. I told him I believed I could help him, but it would mean he would have to make changes, some of which might not be comfortable. He would need to challenge what he believed about how he needed to live, pay attention to all of his feelings (not just anger) before doing things, sort out what was most important to him, and make sure his behavior was in line with those goals. He liked the idea of being able to take action himself rather than just vent to me or wait for me to tell him something brilliant that would magically change him. But more importantly he sensed that there was something deeper going on than just occasional angry outbursts. He knew there was something off about needing to have everything a certain way. He was both tired of it and curious about it.

While his drive made him impatient in our work at times, it was also a source of strength that helped him persevere in facing his challenges. We'll follow Frank in his work to deal with his anger and rigidity to see what he actually did to become a healthier compulsive.

.

CHAPTER FOUR

~

Step 1: Identify Your Story to Develop Insight

Only wisdom based on self-understanding, not piety, will save us.[1]

—Evolutionary biologist Edward O. Wilson

The first step in becoming a healthier compulsive is to become aware of the story you've told yourself about your world and the underlying strategy you've developed to deal with that story. Without being aware of it, when you were quite young you began to tell yourself a story about what it took to survive or to be loved. You developed your own strategy based on that story, and that strategy has determined how healthy or unhealthy you are as a compulsive. A basic narrative template for most compulsives is a story of a hero or heroine who, due to some emergency, gets diverted from his or her true calling, and ends up going in circles trying to get back to it. A common and condensed example of this kind of story and ensuing strategy is: "If I'm not perfect, I won't be loved and I'll be alone. So, I need to use whatever skills I have to try to be perfect."

If you understand your motivations for being overly compulsive, and question whether they are necessary, the behavioral changes you make will be more sustainable. If you're aware that you feel you need to use your energy to compensate for low self-esteem or cover guilt, and you question this strategy, you'll be more likely to stop overextending yourself. If you become aware that you overplan to try to avoid mistakes because mistakes lead to rejection, you'll have an easier time living in the moment. If you're aware that you told yourself a story that said you have to be extraordinarily productive to be acceptable, you'll be less likely to use a workaholic strategy.

When you become aware of your story and your strategy, you have more options. If you can recognize the strategy you developed that leads to the compulsive behavior you're about to engage in, it's easier to stop it: "Oh yeah. I know what that's about and where it leads. I've been there before and I don't have to go there again."

Most compulsives use a very narrow strategy to get by in life. Especially when faced with a problem, you may tend to tighten up when you really need to loosen up. This rigid strategy may feel secure, but it actually limits the possibility of realizing your strengths as a driven person.

Is your story true? It may have been true ten, thirty, fifty years ago. Is it still true that you will be alone if you aren't a high achiever? Is it true that you can only be good if you are rigid? Is it true that you can feel good only if you win that prize? Is it really true that if you "waste" a minute relaxing, you won't meet your goals?

Security: How Good Is Good Enough?

Security is the deep sense that we're safe from irreparable physical and emotional harm, and that we're connected to others. Some of the strategies that driven people adopt to feel more secure are proving they're virtuous, being perfect, planning so as to avoid catastrophes and criticism, and attaining achievement. To some extent this is natural. Estimable acts do bring self-esteem, and with self-esteem comes a sense that we can withstand attacks and that we're worthy of connection with others.

The problem with these strategies is that many compulsive people set their expectations for "goodness" unrealistically high. As *desirable* goals, these expectations are meaningful and helpful. But as goals that are *necessary* to achieve to feel secure, they're more often self-defeating.

A healthier approach is to think of ourselves as "good enough" and achievements beyond that as icing on the cake.

Thinking in terms of being "good enough" helps us to achieve basic self-acceptance that's sustainable. Basic self-acceptance is the belief that you are fundamentally good, aside from what you might or might not achieve. Self-acceptance leads to a more resilient sense of security, one that is less vulnerable to inevitable mistakes, criticism, and events that are out of our control.

Perfectionism is a tempting strategy for people who are compulsive. It's black and white and seems virtuous. "Good enough," on the other hand, has shades of gray, and feels uncomfortably messy. It presents unknowns that someone who is compulsive may find hard to tolerate. But it leads to far fewer problems than those of perfectionism.

Accepting ourselves as "good enough," however, gives us the freedom to acknowledge the places we can grow or improve without having to be defensive, which is actually a more admirable and lovable trait. In fact, making an honest assessment of ourselves, including the acknowledgment of foibles, can actually increase self-respect when we have a basic sense of being good enough.

But how do we get to basic self-acceptance from a strategy based on proving our worth minute to minute? It's not as simple as just talking yourself into it. We'll examine this more in the next chapter when we explore how the experience of connecting with deeper layers of emotion and inner characters helps us to change our sense of ourselves. But for now, question whether the expectations you have set up make you feel more secure or less secure.

The Characters in Your Story

An important aspect of getting to know your story is identifying the characters who act out the drama, the different parts of your personality that have an impact on how you think, feel, and behave. They might not all be visible at first. One or more of them might be taking over the wheel when you don't realize it. Others might be in the backseat screaming directions or sitting mute. Still others might be locked in the trunk, which is unfortunate because the more input and cooperation, the better the ride.

It might seem as if I'm suggesting that you have multiple personality disorder. Not so. I am saying that there are multiple parts to your personality, but I'm not saying you have a disorder. These other characters are simply personifications of networks of neural modules that function together to create a pattern of thinking, feeling, and behavior. These networks exist in everyone—compulsive or not. These figures are completely normal and can be healthy.

They are not so healthy when one particular personality part completely dominates the others, when one set of neural networks overrides all the other neural networks and hijacks the controls. When this happens, that part can make you keep doing things you don't want to, like trying to control other people or working late or letting your anger get the best of you. Other parts are completely excluded, shutting you off from helpful energy and wisdom.

Personifying these networks, imagining what they would look and sound like if they were actual people, is a way of developing more awareness of them.

The Basic Characters: Adult, Parent, and Child

One of the simplest ways to understand your psyche is to map it out into three main parts: the Child (Needs and Desires), the Parent (Shoulds),

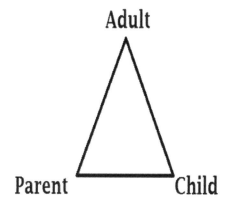

and the Adult (Self-Enlightened Reason).[2] Ideally the Adult is in the driver's seat, with input from the Child about what's going to feel best, and from the Parent about what the right thing to do is: Yes, we'll drive to get ice cream—after we go to the gym.

But any one of these figures can take over control of the personality so that other parts are ignored. Parental Shoulds typically drive unhealthy compulsives, the Adult in the backseat commenting occasionally, trying unsuccessfully to bring some balance and enlightened reason to the trip, and the Child is usually locked in the trunk where its needs and desires can't be heard.

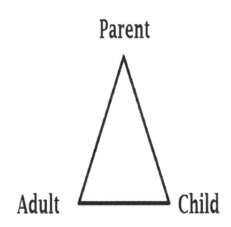

A More Descriptive Map

As the cartographers of yore wrote at the edges of their maps: "Beyond here there be dragons." If you look more closely, there are probably more figures in the car, and describing them with more nuance can be very helpful. A more detailed map of who's in this car offers a much greater possibility of figures—many of them the figures that vex or support compulsives. Instead of describing the dominant aspect of the personality simply as a parental part that's controlling, we could describe it as the Over-controller, the Policeman, the Judge, the Overachiever, the Hero or Heroine, the Martyr, the Warrior, the Prophet, the Artist, the Creator, the Repairman or Repairwoman, Ebenezer Scrooge, and perhaps the favorite of all compulsives, the Saint. All of these figures have their value and their place—but if any of them are too dominant, they can be destructive.

A Compulsive Dethrones the God of Ambition

As an example of someone identifying that they were being driven by a dominant part of the personality, I'll quote Eric Weiner, a journalist and self-confessed grump who went on a worldwide search for happiness.

> Who is my God? No obvious answer springs to mind. Over the years I have been spiritually promiscuous, dabbling in Hinduism, Buddhism, Zoroastrianism, and even occasionally Judaism. None, however would qualify as my full-time faith, my God. Then suddenly his name pops into my mind and His is not a name I expected. Ambition. Yes, that is my God.
>
> When ambition is your God, the office is your temple, the employee handbook your holy book. The sacred drink, coffee, is imbibed five times a day. When you worship Ambition, there is no Sabbath, no day of rest. Every day, you rise early and kneel before the God Ambition, facing in the direction of your PC. You pray alone, always alone, even though others may be present. Ambition is a vengeful God. He will smite those who fail to worship faithfully, but that is nothing compared to what He has in store for the faithful. They suffer the worst fate of all. For it is only when they are old and tired, entombed in the corner office, that the realization hits like a Biblical thunderclap. The God Ambition is a false God and always has been.[3]

Weiner doesn't go on to say whether he chose another God. I suspect he couldn't simply ditch the Ambitious part of himself. But he could choose to aim it more carefully, to clarify what his true Ambition is, separated from the Ambition to simply achieve status.

Dreams

One way to get a better sense of your story, characters, and strategy is to engage with your dreams. Dreams tend to give a picture of what's happening inside of us from a viewpoint that's different from that of the conscious ego, one that is more holistic and takes into consideration other values. They can compensate an unbalanced viewpoint and help to shift how we see ourselves and our situation. Think of the characters in your dreams as aspects of yourself. Do they demonstrate too strong an identity as Police Officer, Victim, Hero, Professor, or Prophet? Observe how they respond to the conflicts and stressors in the dream. Can you see how you do this in your waking life?

Frank Identifies His Story

Over time Frank outlined his story and the characters in it. He was born with a driven personality into a family where rules were paramount. Following rules was the surest way to avoid punishment and shame—the belt from his authoritarian father and the silent treatment from his depressed mother. There were few options to get praise, an essential ingredient for human development. He also recognized that his younger siblings may not have gotten to school on time or stayed out of trouble if he hadn't been on their case. This much of the story was true.

But there were other aspects of the story Frank believed that weren't true.

Even though he didn't see or feel love from his parents, it didn't mean he wasn't loved or that he would be abandoned so easily. The story he told himself—just in the back of his mind—was that he was worthwhile only if he sacrificed himself for everyone else by taking strong leadership. He also extended that story to the rest of the world; he felt he would be punished or shamed by society if he wasn't such a stickler. Simply being a good person wasn't "good enough." But the rest of the world was not like his family.

Frank's strategy to cope with this story was to overcompensate: he not only followed the rules to the "T" himself; he also enforced them harshly on others—siblings, teammates, coworkers, and criminals. This helped him feel secure that he was doing the right thing, that he served a purpose, and that he wouldn't be shamed. But in the long run his strategy only reinforced a sense of conditional acceptance.

Anxiety persists when we avoid the things we fear. Frank avoided his fears of being judged as a slacker by using his natural inclination to work hard. This is the downside of driven people: they can avoid their greatest fears by using their talents, and never have to question their story. Or so it seems for a while.

Frank unearthed his strategy in our conversations about his family, paying attention to the little snippets of memory that turned out to be salient. He began to connect the story of his family with the way he developed to respond to his family's demands. He noticed patterns. He began to compare what he did as a child with what he was doing in the present. He connected how he had responded as a child with how he still responded as an adult. He did this by looking at specific incidents that happened on the job, with his girlfriend, and with his siblings.

He also started to question whether that strategy was working. Eventually he concluded that he no longer needed to be a Bully to stand for The Good.

When we first started mapping out Frank's psyche, the only part of himself that he was aware of was his determination to do the right thing and get other people to do the right thing. This was a strong parental voice, always admonishing him to be good. At times this parental voice took on the tone of a Prophet, telling everyone else in the world what the right thing was for them to do. Because his actual parents weren't available to take their proper role, this Parental Prophet came to dominate Frank's personality as he tried to keep his brothers and sisters in line. This emphasis on guiding others was a large part of his identity.

Another one of George's characteristics that was obvious to everyone but him was his overwhelmingly powerful appearance. He had unconsciously adopted it as part of his strategy. He'd been fascinated with superheroes as a young child, especially Hercules. He'd probably watched the video a hundred times. It was all about the strength—strength that could get out of hand at times when it took over the wheel. It helped him push through difficulties, but it also got him in trouble. As with the coffeepot.

While he felt he was using his strength for good causes, he still came across as a bully. He had little idea how he came across.

There were no clear divisions between the Parent, the Prophet, and Hercules: in a way they were all merged into a character that drove his car. But at other times he could feel one aspect more than the other two.

As is often the case, his Child was in the trunk. Other than the pleasure he took in playing baseball, he had little sense of his Child. But even baseball was serious. Any needs and desires such as play, rest, affection, leisure, and friendship were quickly squashed. His dreams were filled with sad children and abandoned animals. When I pointed out that these were probably aspects of himself, he dismissed my interpretation. But as we noticed more and more hints of this child in him, he began to acknowledge that there might be something to the idea.

He began to observe these characters in action in our sessions and between sessions. He set an intention to notice each time one of these characters took the wheel. He noticed that even his jokes were laced with implied judgment, letting other people know that they weren't hitting the mark. He loved busting people's chops. I pointed it out when he did it with me.

Carrying out this intention to recognize the different parts of his personality and creating a map of his internal characters strengthened his Adult part—his capacity to be more balanced and reasonable in his actions. It also helped him to decide when to listen to the other voices—Parent, Prophet, Hercules, and Child.

Summary

- Take the time to write out the story of your four-act play:
  - what you were born with,
  - the environment you were born into,
  - how you coped with the fit between the two, and
  - whether you continue to use that strategy.
- How does this story and strategy affect your day-to-day life? Try to identify in a detailed way when you use that strategy. Keep a log of as many instances as you can.
- Identify and observe the different parts of your personality: who dominates and who is hidden?
- Question whether the story is accurate and whether the strategy still works.

~

CHAPTER FIVE

Step 2: Engage Emotionally with Deeper Layers of Feeling and Parts of Yourself

Somewhere along the way I realized my heart wasn't driving me—my anger was.

—Richard Pimentel[1]

Step 2 requires two main tools to encourage the transformational experience that emotions can provide:

1. Allow yourself to experience layers of emotion beneath the ones you are aware of.
2. Listen empathically to the characters that embody those emotions.

Allow Yourself to Experience Deeper Layers of Emotion

To move toward the healthier end of the compulsive spectrum, you will need to stop avoiding emotions with busy-ness and instead allow them to flow into consciousness. Once you're aware of what you're feeling, you can decide how to respond to it. If you don't, you'll be driven by forces you aren't aware of.

Emotions are a necessary element in change. If you've become com-pulsive to an unhealthy degree, it's as if your brain is a machine that's become rusty and doesn't function as flexibly as it was designed to. It's stuck in one position. Emotions serve as solvents, lubricating and loos-ening rigidly held positions. To become healthier, you'll need to allow the flow of these natural solvents.

While it is true for everyone that avoiding feelings can make the feelings more disturbing, people who suffer from OCPD are particularly prone to a cycle of negative emotions (which I'll explain shortly) if they don't slow down to deal with them.[2] One explanation for this is that people who are driven have energy and a capacity for intense work that give them a way to avoid their feelings that's socially sanctioned and rewarded. Avoiding emotions may seem beneficial at first, but over time it can lead to a rut of anger, disappointment, and cynicism.

But what does it mean to listen to feelings? It means to allow the feeling to rise into consciousness long enough to really experience it, to understand what's bothering you, to develop the capacity to tolerate the feeling, and to see if there is anything to learn from it. Some do this when speaking with a therapist; some do it when writing or journaling;[3] others do it during periods of intentional introspection focusing on the body as the source of information.[4] For most compulsives, this will need to be deliberate; you're likely to rush into doing rather than feeling, and consequently you miss both disturbing and positive feelings.

Layers of Feelings

Paying attention to emotion will require you to look beneath the emotion that's on the surface to other emotions that may not be so noticeable. What feelings have you put in the trunk of your car? In our efforts to avoid emotion, without knowing it we often try to cover one disturbing feeling by focusing on another feeling that isn't as disturb-ing. For instance, we may focus on our anger to cover feelings that would otherwise leave us feeling too vulnerable, such as fear or sadness. Others who are not comfortable with anger may focus on their anxiety or depression. Urgency may cover helplessness because it leaves you feeling you can do something. Determination may cover shame because it feels like you're being a better person if you work hard.

Until we slow down and pay attention to these deeper levels of feeling, we are oblivious to their effects. We are driven by the underlying feeling that we're not aware of. Frank's anger covered his fear of getting in trouble and experiencing shame, and until he consciously faced his fear and shame, he was always on edge. Someone else might be aware of their fear or shame, but not of a deeper layer of anger or simply assertive energy that feels more disturbing. If you're angry at having to live in a constricted way, but are uncomfortable with that anger, you may focus more on an intense sense of urgency about getting work done. Working harder and harder will not resolve the underlying anger. Allowing yourself to experience your deeper layers of feeling and learning to tolerate them as they slowly diminish or transform is essential to realizing the potential of your driven personality.

Here are six primary emotions and some of their variations that you will need to recognize in yourself. Try to get a felt sense of each of them. Which ones are prominent? Which ones are below the surface for you? Where do you feel them in your body?

Anger
Compulsives have a special love-hate relationship with anger. They can't live with it and they can't live without it. You may pump it up to prove you're right, but you may also feel guilty for having it. Anger and resentment often arise for driven people when they feel they're being controlled, and when it seems that other people are getting away with not being so controlled. They also get angry when they feel others are blocking their progress.

One danger for compulsives is that anger may feel completely justified, as if expressing anger is the moral thing to do. People with road rage feel that they should be teaching the other person a lesson. Righteous indignation often spoils relations between compulsives and the people around them. Their anger can lead them to be aggressive and even violent, or it can take its toll in less obvious ways. For example, suppressed anger may turn into righteousness, judgment, resentment, and stubbornness—all of which may lead you to indulge in passive-aggressive behavior, withholding the things that you know other people want or expect from you. Frank could be direct with some people, but with other people—like his siblings—he would just stop talking to them in order to silently punish them. While compulsives usually try to avoid anger, their strategy can lead to outbursts.[5]

Hate is a variant of anger that compulsives often find confusing. While it's not unusual to have passing feelings of hate even for someone we love, hate may not fit in with how we like to think of ourselves. We may rely on a self-image of being kind or loving, and so attempt to deny feeling hate, rather than acknowledge it as a passing feeling, or one that exists alongside other feelings.

Dealing with anger may require more direct, active, and conscious use of healthy assertion before it gets out of control. It's also important to deal with anger consciously in order not to get depressed. If you don't deal with your anger consciously, you may turn it against yourself.

Sadness, Depression, Powerlessness, and Futility

Given the standards they set for who they should be and what they should be able to accomplish and control, it's not unusual for people who are driven to begin to feel that it's completely impossible to do what they feel they should. This can lead to feelings of powerlessness and futility, and to depression.

If we think of low mood as a natural compensation for unrealistic expectations,[6] as a message from our psyche, we can learn from it and adjust our expectations. But instead we may try to use perfection and productivity to avoid or cure our depression. It's like running as fast as we can to get away from fatigue. No wonder we get tired.

The solution is to acknowledge limitations and sit with the feelings of loss that may come when we admit we don't have as much control as we imagined.

Shame and Guilt

In order to get children to comply and be good citizens, many parents, teachers, and religious figures induce feelings of guilt and shame in them. Guilt is the sense that one has made a mistake; shame is the sense that one is fundamentally bad, inadequate, or broken in some way. Shame is a deeper problem, but either guilt or shame may underlie the intense feeling that we need to accomplish tasks. Some children begin to make themselves feel guilt and shame to preempt others from criticizing, punishing, or rejecting them. In other cases there may have been no threat of being shamed from outside, but the children compared themselves to those around them and, feeling they should achieve as much as their caretakers did, created their own critical voice, thinking this would help them achieve what those around them had achieved. These feelings may or may not be conscious, but they are often what drive people to use work and achievements to try to prove their worth or goodness, and to leave guilt and shame behind. It's better to face into these feelings, accept appropriate responsibility and our own limits, and move toward releasing inappropriate guilt and shame.

Fear and Anxiety
Beneath the sense of determination and urgency that many compulsives are usually aware of often lies a deep fear of not measuring up, and consequently of being punished or rejected. This fear, however, often isn't conscious, and it produces a more generalized and chronic sense of foreboding and dread. They don't know what it is they fear. Many theorists attribute compulsive behavior entirely to this sort of anxiety. According to this hypothesis, accomplishing tasks is simply their way of trying to silence anxiety. It's far more complicated than that, but this strategy is certainly part of the equation.

Like many people, compulsives can feel anxious about being unloved. But what many compulsives feel more directly is pressure to measure up to imagined standards of morality and productivity. This is both because of the environment they were raised in and because of the skills they had at their disposal to deal with the felt threat of being abandoned.

Many compulsives avoid anxiety by trying to control the future and trying not to make any mistakes. This can be adaptive in a practical way, but very destructive emotionally. It's better to learn to find a way to handle inevitable roadblocks and personal errors than to spend your life trying to prevent them. As Harvard psychologist Daniel Gilbert points out in his book *Stumbling on Happiness*,[7] we're far better at handling disasters than we imagine we will be.

If you tend to obsess or procrastinate, this is probably also caused by avoiding emotion. Not wanting to feel emotion can lead us to vacillate between conflicting approaches, trying to avoid one uncomfortable feeling by substituting its opposite. But it turns out that the substitute emotion is no more comfortable than the first and we simply go back and forth between the two, never taking any action that would allow a sense of relief.

Sometimes people use work to avoid feelings in a generalized way; the activity they engage in isn't specifically related to the feeling they are trying to avoid. But sometimes it's symbolic and very specific: they transfer the inner issue to an external one that resembles it, trying to solve an inner, emotional problem as if it were an outer, practical one, without being aware of doing so. Frank did this when the city council cut their personal days. While it was true that he didn't like what the council did, in his fight with them he was also trying to fight back against his own tendency to tyrannize himself. He projected the way he controlled himself onto the council.

Someone else may try to fix something that feels messy, unresolved, or out of control inside of them by trying to clean it up, resolve it, or control it on the outside. For instance, if you feel shame about who you are, something you've done, or something that has happened to you, you may feel as if you're dirty inside, and you may start cleaning your kitchen to try to get rid of the feeling that you yourself are dirty. This way you never deal with the emotion that's calling for attention. You're only distracting yourself from it. This is also known as displacement, and we will revisit it in the section on psychological growth.

Discontent

As much as compulsives may avoid emotion, they can also get stuck in it. There are many reasons for this. One is that they don't let themselves fully experience the deepest layers of their emotion. It doesn't flow as it would normally, diminishing with time and acknowledgment. Another reason is that because they are perfectionistic, they won't allow themselves to be happy until everything, and I mean everything, is fixed. Whether it's a toenail that needs trimming or world peace that needs winning, compulsives find it hard to rest until their issues are resolved. Because they're good at tolerating frustration and delaying gratification, this can go on for a very long time—for some, their entire life. This is why compulsives often have a reputation for being constantly grumpy. It's why unhealthy compulsives develop the habit of discontent.

It might seem obvious that you're discontent. What may not be obvious is both how persistent it is, and how necessary it feels. Ongoing discontent should be a message that something is off inside of us, that

our response to problems on the outside is not effective. But it's usually interpreted as a message to try to control what's outside of us. No
wonder it never changes.

In order not to be perpetually grumpy, you'll need to begin by observing and acknowledging this habit of discontent. Once you see how
it dominates your emotional life, you will need to accept that things
will never be perfect and let go of the need to have them fixed now. To
accept does not mean giving in and surrendering; it just means that you
let go of the need to have it resolved now. Letting go gets easier if you
have something else to hold onto. We'll tackle that in the next chapter, but for now, you can start asking what might be more meaningful
and fulfilling than trying to make everything perfect now.

Desire
Many compulsives have lost track of what they desire, and instead rely
entirely on what they think they *should* do for direction. While this
might seem admirable, it can be destructive in the long run. It might
seem to you that your desires are destructive or dangerous, but in the
long term you end up spending life mechanically checking off boxes
rather than living in a fulfilling way. Doing things because you desire
to do them puts you back on track to a life of meaning. Frank needed to
remember that he wanted to serve justice and to mentor his siblings. It
was natural to him. It became problematic when he felt that he needed
to do it because he should do it; he became overbearing.

Trying to live a life based entirely on "shoulds" without some direction from desire also tends to backfire. Since desires never go away
completely, it's best that we find truly fulfilling ways to satisfy them, or
else they find expression in unhealthy ways.

Feelings as a Source of Wisdom and Direction

Avoiding feelings not only creates a cycle of felt inadequacy and overextending; it also cuts you off from a source of direction and wisdom.
Each of these feelings can serve as a warning sign that something is out
of balance.

At times it is wise to *consciously* put certain feelings aside and do
the practical or moral thing, but over time this strategy becomes an

unconscious habit and erodes a mindful connection with a more effective guide to what's most important. We like to imagine that we can use reason as our sole source of direction—like Mr. Spock from *Star Trek*. But the reality is that it's really feeling that organizes and directs our behavior—whether we want to admit it or not. As neuroscience researcher Anthony Damasio argues convincingly in his book *Descartes' Error*,[8] we exist not because we think, rather we exist because we feel. He challenges seventeenth-century philosopher René Descartes' famous pronouncement that has guided much Western thought: "I think, therefore I am." Reason without emotional guidance is aimless and meaningless.

Finding direction from feeling will be essential when we begin to clarify meaning in Step 3.

A Word of Caution

Be forewarned: allowing yourself to feel emotions and not cover them with compulsive behavior will make you uncomfortable—perhaps even terrified—at first. It may feel as if you're betraying deeply held values. But if it does make you uncomfortable to slow down and feel, that's probably a good sign that you're moving in the right direction. Exposing yourself to the feelings you've dreaded for years, if not decades, will eventually help you get comfortable with them. When you're able to let go for a little while, you may start to feel like you've forgotten something or let go of something and the dread starts to come back in. Many people experience this in their anxiety dreams. Identify the fear: it won't go away quickly, but if you name the fear, in time those feelings will not be as threatening. Think of it as going through withdrawal.

All of this needs to be done with compassion and understanding. Using shame or punishment will only continue the cycle.

Empathically Connect with the
Different Aspects of Your Personality

One important way to access feelings is to connect empathically with the parts of your personality that embody your feelings. For instance—and all these combinations could be switched around—the Child may embody desire and hope and excitement, while the Parent embodies anger and judgment, and the Hero embodies determination. Unhealthy compulsives tend to have a very limited sense of identity and therefore a limited range of feelings: certain parts of the personality dominate and other parts are ignored. This limits access to the feelings those personality parts carry. To remedy this, you'll need to get to know the cast of characters in your story and welcome their feelings.

Consciously and intentionally using imagination can help us to understand how these characters feel and why they behave as they do. While this may sound a little odd, having an imaginary dialogue with some of these characters, and writing out the dialogue as it occurs, both requires and develops a strong executive function. It's not crazy. Further, we do have research to support the efficacy of this sort of dialogue in regulating affect, developing a balanced connection with our emotions.[9] Such dialogue can make allies of enemies, and help them to take their proper role in a healthier story.

There are many ways to describe these parts of the personality, and how you describe them doesn't matter. What is important is to begin to get an empathic sense of why some parts feel the need to dominate and others feel they need to hide. All of these parts have both positive and negative potential: at best their energy and wisdom serve as guides; at worst they completely take over and hijack your car.

The problem for many compulsives is that they're unaware of these other parts. Their sense of "I" is limited to that of a very reasonable Adult ego, as if it has complete control of the wheel, when in fact its choices are often dictated by parts of their psyche that the Adult ego has little connection with. The parts that we don't recognize can become far less reasonable and exert far more influence than we'd like to admit. Figures such as an angry Hercules, a frightened child, or an authoritarian parent often take over the wheel as part of a strategy to feel more secure. A healthier way to get to your destination is to get input from these figures rather than have them at the wheel. Other figures that have been repressed by the dominating figure such as a more poised hero, a playful child, or a wise old man can provide energy, direction, and meaning.

On the one hand, if we are unconscious of inner figures, we are driven recklessly. But on the other hand, without trusting some guidance from within, we may find ourselves quite nervous. Even the

"Adult" needs to have guidance from the child, parent, or any other figures it discovers within. On its own the Adult has no real sense of direction. It has a method (reason) but no motivation (passion or desire).

Any map that leads to a healthier life needs to extend beyond the territory of the ego, to aspects of the psyche that, while powerful, have not been conscious before. Without awareness of and assistance from the rest of the psyche, life is anxiety provoking. Yet this is how unhealthy compulsives live. Imagine being president of a large country with no cabinet or advisors to support you. It's lonely at the top.

Frank Lets Go

Frank had to do more than just figure things out in a detached way. He also had to feel the things he had avoided feeling and mourn that which could not be changed. After I met with Frank for several sessions, we started practicing slowing down and paying attention to what he was feeling. It actually became a joke between us. I'd ask him playfully, "Where are you rushing off to today, Frank?" He'd give me a squeamish smile and sit back on the couch, remembering to settle in and see what was going on inside. This wasn't easy for him. It usually meant that he had to face a feeling—and a reality—that something was out of his control. The things he had to let go of ranged broadly, from setting the city council straight to getting his younger brother to stop using drugs. He saw the pattern. He tried to control so that he wouldn't feel powerless and so that he wouldn't feel guilty about not doing whatever he possibly could do to help.

He felt that he was giving up on something very important when he let go of the battle over personal days. He also acknowledged that that battle mirrored something inside of him—he never let himself have days off—and he was transferring the inner issue onto the outer world. He didn't let himself have days off because his identity was so invested in his image of himself as a hero fighting for The Good.

But this was just one example of many times when he needed to let go of control and notice what he felt. He noticed that the layers of feeling beneath anger were a fear of being shamed and of feeling powerless. But he also learned that it was OK to feel anger, and that if he allowed himself to be aware of it and express it appropriately, he was actually less likely to explode. He also learned to see the fear beneath his anger: fear that he'd attack himself for not being a guardian of The Good, fear that he would feel shame for not taking responsibility, and fear that he would be found lacking.

His old strategy had a side effect: it left him angrier and more resentful. It felt entirely justified, and he imagined it was effective. But his energy and natural sense of integrity had been hijacked by his resentment for having to be so constricted and by his resentment at others for not following the rules as adamantly as he did.

Many times I would ask Frank what he felt and he would tell me what he thought. He eventually learned to tell the difference.

In one session he spoke about being so busy that he really didn't know what he had been feeling. I asked him what he might feel if he weren't so busy. "Guilt" popped out with no hesitation. For what? Not doing everything he could. Why was everything his responsibility? We took this a level deeper and he realized that the idea that something was out of his control seemed truly intolerable. He feared it would be just too depressing. He learned to sort out real responsibility from the habitual guilt he always felt. He learned to tolerate that some things were out of his control. This meant not reacting to these feelings by working overtime and not constantly going to his siblings' apartments to check up on them or do things for them. These feelings slowly diminished over time as he exposed himself to them.

Perhaps the hardest and most important emotion for Frank was vulnerability—which he experienced when he let go of control. This was his greatest fear, and to him it smacked of going soft. When I pointed out how challenging it was to "go soft," Frank got it: not being in charge took more courage than staying in battle mode all the time. To follow through on this, he made an effort to pressure his siblings less, and instead face the feeling that he would be shamed if they had a problem. As he let himself experience his vulnerability, he began to feel less afraid. As he felt the vulnerability and fear, he began to develop greater capacity to empathize with others.

He appeared to care about his body: he worked out regularly and was in great shape. But it was really a master/slave relationship. He pushed his body, too. He let it know who was in control. He didn't sleep much, and he carried a lot of physical tension. He didn't go to the doctor.

His blood pressure was through the roof. Being driven was going to drive him to the grave. When he finally did see a doctor, it was part of a larger shift of attention from what was happening outside of him to what was happening inside of him.

During our sessions I asked him to also pay attention to his body—where he felt anger and where he felt fear. He began to notice the tension in his shoulders when he was afraid, just before it turned to anger. He noticed that he felt better when he felt his center of gravity lower in his body, not in his shoulders and head. He started to develop a sense of a core that wasn't thrown off by what other people did so much.

I asked him to start to notice feelings other than anger, fear, and shame. He could detect brief moments of pleasure, happiness, relief, and calm, but these seemed irrelevant to him. "What good are these feelings? They don't get any work done! What's the point?!"

"Great question," I told him. "What is the point of anything you do or feel? Do you know?" He looked at me a little suspiciously, as if I were trying to trick him. We'll continue this in the next chapter.

He also engaged with the characters that he had identified in his story. The Parent felt extraordinary responsibility and a fear of failing in its duties. Similarly his Prophet, like the ones he had heard about in church, was under pressure from God to preach his message—or else. Like the actual mythological character, his personal version of Hercules was always trying to make up for his fits of anger. His Child was depressed and lonely, afraid to come out for fear of getting in trouble, if he allowed himself to play spontaneously.

Acknowledging and welcoming the feelings of each of these characters was a reach for Frank. It was a little too "woo-woo" to him. But over time he did develop an attitude toward these other parts of himself that allowed him to see who had been driving him, and to let the Child have more say about where he drove.

Summary

- Break the cycle of emotional avoidance and overextending: stop using productivity and perfection as ways to avoid anger, depression, anxiety, or shame. Take the risk of not working as long, and of not making everything perfect.

- Sit down for ten minutes to notice what you feel. Don't multitask. This deserves your full attention. Writing will help you to focus and stay on track.
- Visualize all the tasks you have before you as a pile or a mountain: what emotions arise?
- Fill in the blank:
  ◦ If I don't keep doing things, I will feel _____.
  ◦ If I don't achieve, _____ will happen.
- Identify the emotion you're trying to avoid: Anger? Fear? Shame? Powerless? Powerful? Helplessness? Sinfulness? Inferiority? Arrogance? Sadness? What have you been dreading? A fear of a loss of identity as perfect, good, diligent, or likable? Allow any of these to rise into consciousness and see what there is to learn from them.
- Identify which of these feelings are on the top layer and which ones are underneath.
- Note when you feel most compulsive or just uncomfortable: When there's no structured task to do? When you go on vacation? When you're getting close to another person? When you start to let yourself go and have fun? When you fear you will fail?
- Accept feelings of limitation and set realistic standards for what you can accomplish without paying too much of an emotional price.
- Develop your capacity to speak about feelings, not just thoughts. The two are not the same. The next time someone asks you what you feel, don't say what you think.
- Draw a map that shows the different parts of your personality and which ones dominate. Get to know what it feels like when each one is in control.
- Empathically understand why certain parts of your personality insist on perfection. Imagine speaking with them about it. Reassure them that they don't need to do this. Develop a connection with them.
- Personify the strategy that's been driving your car. Has it been a frightened child white-knuckling it at the wheel? A rigid judge? A frantic achiever? A resentful perfectionist? Once you identify him or her, imagine talking to that person kindly and saying that it's time for you to take over the wheel. Let the person know that you will still listen to him or her.

- Set an intention to have the Adult behind the wheel, but also to have the Adult take into consideration the needs and aspirations of all the parts of the personality.
- Stop feeding the beast. Develop an intention to slow down and note feelings as often as you can. Remember, you're in the fourth act of your life story now, and you can choose whether to sustain the habits you developed when you were younger or find a better way to honor the things you're driven to do.

CHAPTER SIX

~

Step 3: Cultivate Meaning

Clarify Your Aspirations and Set Your Priorities

The most important thing is to remember the most important thing.

—Attributed to Suzuki Roshi

The real crisis of the unhealthy compulsive is the loss of purpose. The evidence might seem to contradict this at first, since compulsives are so goal oriented. But the goals they aim for have lost the soul and spirit of the original intention.[1] They've missed the point and forgotten the real destination. Backing up enough to remember the point and then finding the most meaningful place to put your energy are indispensable for recovery.

Let's remember that the word "compulsive" derives from the Latin "compelled," and refers to an internal force, urge, or drive that is difficult to resist. Like the word pulse, it also has the sense of beating, as the heart does, and hence alive. So, we could think of this step as reconnecting with (com) your life force (pelled).

You will need to ask not just what problems from the past led to your personality style, but also where your passions have wanted to go; not just "Why am I this way?" but also "What am I this way *for?*" What is the original urge that you feel compelled to respond to?

Recall our exploration of the sources of the driven personality in chapter 2: your tendencies are not just defensive reactions to rigid or neglectful parenting. They are also part of your disposition: natural urges to accomplish life goals. You are driven not just because you felt insecure or inadequate, but also because you had a deep desire to be creative, to master problems, to produce things that would be valuable to the world, or any of the many other purposes that driven people feel passionate about.

Too often psychology pathologizes human struggle rather than understanding the urges beneath it. Most theorists tend to attribute compulsive tendencies to fear or anger.[2] They commonly say that compulsives are trying to sublimate pathological tendencies—that is, to take the energy of unwanted instinctual tendencies and raise it to socially acceptable levels through compulsive behavior. This is backward. Unhealthy compulsives have taken healthy urges and made them unhealthy. Healthy compulsives use their compulsive energy and talents in a healthy way. It's not that we turn something dysfunctional into something acceptable. Rather we become adapted and healthy when we find the original positive intent inherent in those compulsive urges and find a constructive way to live them out, rather than enlisting their energies in repetitive and meaningless behaviors.

Certainly fear and anger play a role. But they are not the sole cause or the deepest source. As Carl Jung wrote, "The neurotic is ill not because he has lost his old faith, but because he has not yet found a new form for his finest aspirations."[3] The problem that unhealthy compulsives have is not that they have an irresistible inner drive or urge, but that they are not conscious of where that inner urge or drive really wants to go.

Reclaiming Original Goals

So the next task to become healthier is to discern what your urges compel you to accomplish. These urges were not clear when you were young, nor did Nature lay them down explicitly. But look deeply enough and you'll get a general sense of direction, a sense of what's most important to you. That urge may have many paths for realization.

Some of your purpose may be found through becoming aware of deeper levels of emotion and personality parts. Look beneath shame and fear and you'll probably find desires. Use your imagination and ask the personality parts that have been neglected or dismissed where they want to go, and you'll probably find aspirations. These will give you a larger map to work from, one that shows where you really want to go, not just the places you wanted to avoid.

In a study of the treatment of OCPD, psychologist Jacques Barber, then at the University of Pennsylvania, found that one intervention successful in reducing perfectionism was to identify the core relational conflict the patient had, the narrative theme that ran throughout his or her life, and then to uncover what the patient really wanted to get that led to the conflict.[4] The client could then find a better way to achieve that goal.

Unhealthy compulsives often grew up in environments that created a core relational conflict between two fundamental urges: wanting to be loved and wanting to be one's authentic self, with its intrinsic drives. They felt forced to enlist their talents to be loved or accepted, and lost sight of their authentic self and what they really wanted to accomplish. Getting healthier requires that we recall or discover our original goals and ways to pursue them while still maintaining good relationships.

This doesn't mean pleasing everyone. But still, even the most ardent compulsive needs good relationships to be healthy, balanced, and ful-filled. Typically, however, in their determination to make the world a better place for people, compulsives lose track of their actual relation-ships with those people.

I'll have more to say about this in Part III when discussing the fulcrum issue of people, but let me give two brief examples. Let's imagine a mother or father who, out of fear of not providing well for the family financially, spends most of the time earning money to support them, and little or no time actually being with them. If that parent looks beneath the fear, he or she may find that the original desire was to create a place where the parents and children could enjoy close supportive relationships.

Another example would be of someone whose personality has been taken over by a Judge part, a part that insists that everyone follow the rules exactly and criticizes them if they don't. This Judge part ends up oppressing herself and everyone around her. If she asks that Judge why she is the way she is, she might realize that she first set those standards so that people could lead healthy, happy lives, free of oppression. Much of the insistence on rules and doing the right thing that compulsives engage in originally emerged from a desire to help everyone live freely, but that desire too often becomes oppressive.

Frank Considers What's Important

"What's the point?" Frank had asked me.

"Exactly!" I responded, "What is the point?" Without my prompting him Frank had asked probably the most important question every driven person needs to ask.

After a particularly difficult week Frank admitted to me that he'd just like to find a little peace. Part of him was tired of the constant urgency. Even though he had put in his twenty years and was entitled to a retirement package, we both knew that wasn't going to happen anytime soon. In fact, it might never be time for him to retire. Frank had too much energy for that, but it was important for him to decide consciously what to do with that energy.

Frank had to choose his battles. He couldn't get everyone to do the right thing. But at the same time, Hercules, the Parent, and the Prophet were all real parts of his personality that needed to be taken into consideration. So we explored what the original urge was for, before it had become rigid.

I asked him why it was important to get everyone to do the right thing in the first place.

"So that no one gets hurt."

"And why is that important?"

He looked at me like I had three heads. "Come on doc, isn't that obvious?"

"Maybe not. Why is it important to you?"

He told me that he'd seen people suffer and wanted to prevent as much of that as possible.

"So, it's 'cause you care about people?"

Again the blank stare. "Duh!"

"OK, but how do you fit that with how you actually treat them? Like that officer you chewed out last week, or your sister whom you made feel really guilty for overspending her budget? Don't they count?"

He gave me a look we had both come to recognize, which said, "For once you're right, but I don't want to give it to you."

Everything mattered to Frank, but he had forgotten why it all mattered. Retracing his steps, he realized that some of his original insistence on doing the right thing came out of a concern for his brother and sisters. Even though he was actually only their brother, he had a strong parental part to his personality and it wasn't going away. It was an important part of him that informed what he wanted to do with his life. The goal that came out of this part of him was to help and guide. He felt a need to teach them to work together as a family: they each had to pull their weight and do the right thing. There wasn't a lot of room for error. Helping them understand this felt deeply important to him, not just a reaction to anxiety.

This Parental part was intensified by the Prophet part. It wasn't just his siblings he cared about and felt a need to instruct. He had a larger concern about how all people were supposed to behave, and that concern had grown rigid and judgmental. He punished people to try to get them to do the right thing. The means now superseded the end. The strategy was based on an old story that people needed to be punished to behave well. This realization led to a shift in priorities. He still stood for his principles, but he started to question how he had been trying to achieve them.

He had other motivations that weren't obvious at first. His efforts to be good at everything he did were part of an intrinsic desire to grow as a person. All the energy for growth had gone into trying to get people to behave decently and into being a better baseball player. These weren't bad goals, but they didn't really satisfy the deeper urge to become a human being who was both happy and caring.

To his surprise, he found that that he was able to get into this whole idea of shaping his personality. Therapy wasn't such a drag anymore. He wasn't a self-help sort of guy, but he did recognize an old feeling, one from his childhood, about being driven to be the best he could be. It was as if he remembered something he had always known, but had never known consciously. He clarified his goals: caring about people and developing his own personality. This required not just words and ideas, but concrete action.

But he also realized that buried deeply underneath his desire to be a good person and to get people to act decently was also a desire to simply feel that he was basically good and to be at peace with himself, to not always be on guard against being accused of having fallen short. His intrinsic desire to grow had been hijacked to prove that he was basically good. It had been exhausting because he could never allow himself to rest in a sense that he was OK—he was perpetually trying to prove it to himself. He could never have said it before, but one of the reasons that he was so adamant about people behaving well was that he wanted to be treated well himself. George's ongoing challenge was to value both of these desires: to accept himself as he was, but also to honor his desire to grow.

Summary

- Draw a pie chart of the things that are most important to you. Now draw a pie chart of how you actually spend your time and energy.
- What was important to you when you were younger? How has that changed? Identify the original urge that has been hijacked by fear. What is it that you really want to accomplish?
- What purpose or purposes would give your life the most fulfillment now?
- How would you spend your time if you were living your life based on those priorities?

~

CHAPTER SEVEN

Step 4: Take Action

Commit to Behavior That Honors Your Aspirations

Action is the antidote to despair.

—Joan Baez

Action expresses priorities.

—Mohandas Gandhi

It's time for the Adult to take the wheel. Once you have a more accurate story and a more effective strategy, a better connection with your feelings and personality parts, and a clearer sense of your purpose, you will need to honor your aspirations with your behavior. You won't be able to achieve the progress you want just by changing how you think. While insight creates the conditions for change, action provides the fuel that makes it happen. While feelings often change after insight about what's happening inside, some feelings will change only after you change your behavior.

What behavior do you need to let go of? What is it that you actually do that causes problems? Start by identifying exactly where you cross over the line in your behavior. Once you can identify that, you'll need to set intentions not to step over the line. Maybe it's OK to work until 7:00 p.m., but not at all on the weekend. Maybe it's OK to make suggestions to other people but not criticize them. Maybe it's OK to perfect your meals but not your clothing. Not so easy, but an indispensable start.

Here's why: when you stop unhealthy behavior, you'll probably start to feel the emotions you've tried to avoid feeling most of your life. Exposing yourself to the things you fear eventually leads to greater tolerance of them and less need to engage in unhealthy compulsive behavior. As you change old behaviors for new ones, notice what you feel when you don't give in to the urge to repeat old behaviors. Is this a feeling that you've been avoiding? Know that each time you change your behavior, even small actions, you also develop new neural connections that override habitual ones—neural connections that with time will also make the new behavior more comfortable.

It helps to replace old behaviors with new ones. It's important that the new behaviors you choose lead to a more balanced life. Whether behavior is healthy or unhealthy is based less on how driven it is, and more on what that behavior might exclude from your personality and your life.[1] There's nothing wrong with a passionate devotion to building the world's most magnificent birdhouses, but if it means you isolate and don't take care of yourself, it is a problem.

Turn the problem of your compulsiveness on its head: enlist your capacity for hard work to honor your priorities and deepest goals. One of the reasons that people who are driven become unhealthy compulsives is that their repetitive behavior—be it work, repairing, planning, or controlling—doesn't really value their true priorities, and so it's never fulfilling. It's like a dog chasing its tail. The repetitive behavior feels like a safer substitute for the more meaningful pursuits that might carry risk. But the repetitive behavior never satisfies.

The goal is to find a better way to honor the aspirations you've always had, taking back the energy for them that had been hijacked to feel more secure, and redirecting this energy more consciously.

Frank Makes Some Changes

As his old strategy and new priorities became clearer, Frank began to set specific intentions to make changes in his life.

After years of arguing with his brother and sisters he made it a point not to tell them what to do or how to live their lives. It was hard to watch them do things that he felt were mistakes. But with time he began to realize it was much more effective to support them than to badger them. He honored his original urge—to help them be happy and safe. He learned to become a Brother, rather than a Parent, for the first time in his life.

At the office he focused on what he could control rather than what he couldn't control. He couldn't control the budget, but he could stick up for his buddies when they were treated unfairly. He focused more on mentoring and less on punishing. While he lost none of his determination to investigate criminals, he quit wasting energy where it wasn't effective. The Prophet learned to take direction from the Adult.

He set intentions to act with a different sort of strength; his Hercules had new challenges more appropriate for a man his age—including restraint. He learned to pause whenever he noticed he was getting angry. Feeling angry was fine; acting impulsively on the anger was not. While it remained an ongoing challenge for him, he did start to find ways to say what he was angry about before acting angrily. He learned to ask himself two questions in that pause: Will I feel better or worse if I do that? and, Will this get me what I want? The thoughtful pause required a much more nuanced use of his strength.

While he didn't use this language, he made it a point to find time for the Child to come out and play. He started to take his vacation days with his girlfriend. He joined a baseball league. He made more jokes. These actions also served to honor his effort to have respect for himself. Spending his time not working was an active way to say, "You're OK, Frank. You don't need to work constantly to prove yourself." He also honored his intention to respect his own basic goodness by making it a point not to make disparaging remarks about himself to himself. That in itself served as a constant reminder of his basic goodness.

Overall Frank let go of his rigid need to set the world and himself straight, and he began to engage more in activities that offered longer-lasting gratifications. He found changing himself to be satisfying, and he found it more satisfying to care for people personally and directly rather than in theory. After all, that was the point, that was the original intention underlying his need to be a Bully for The Good in the first place.

Summary

Following are general guidelines and, just as examples, specific suggestions. Some may not apply. Tailor the suggestions to your own priorities.

- Make a list of your specific compulsive behaviors (both small and large) that you don't need to do to sustain yourself or your family. Set an intention to refrain from these behaviors and to be open to feelings that might rush in when you don't engage in them. Be aware of the dread or anxiety without reacting to it. Learn to tolerate anxiety.
- Give yourself a checkmark or points—at least mentally, if not literally on paper or on your phone—each time you don't engage in these behaviors and each time you become aware of the feeling behind it.
- Give particular attention to the behaviors that feel urgent. Slow down. Resist responding with urgency unless it's absolutely necessary.
  - Don't check your phone or email unless you really have to.
  - Take as many opportunities as you can to practice walking more slowly.
- Spend less time working. Prioritize people, leisure, creativity, or pleasure over work to the extent that you can.
  - If you've been neglecting your family for work, plan activities that honor your purpose in having a family and that you would enjoy.
  - Don't limit your reading to professional books, articles, or websites. Do start a novel that you enjoy.
  - Experiment with savoring other areas of life that had been excluded.
- Stop controlling and start letting go.
  - Find as many opportunities as you can to let someone else take over some of the work and decisions. Delegate. Give yourself appreciation each time you do. The new goal is not to control the world but to feel better.
  - Quit being the world's police. Let people get away with things as often as is reasonable.

- ◦ Find as many ways that you can to compliment people, and enjoy doing it.
- ◦ Don't punish the guy in the car that cut you off by tailgating. Do enjoy your body relaxing rather than preparing for conflict.
- ◦ Don't try to dress perfectly. Do enjoy the freedom of not worrying about what people think.
- Stop clinging to money. Adopt other values.
  - ◦ Make a small donation the next time someone asks, just as an experiment. How does it feel? The point is less about the money and more about letting go of control.
  - ◦ Don't check to see if the coupons applied every time you go to the supermarket.
- Be less efficient and give yourself points each time you do. It's probably more efficient over time to let go in order to get to your desired destination.
  - ◦ Don't run for the train. Do practice deep breathing as you walk slowly for the next train instead.
- Stop leaning forward and holding so much tension in your body. Set an intention to drop your shoulders and adopt a more relaxed posture. Enjoy relaxing.
- Find as many opportunities as you can to allow yourself to be imperfect. Give yourself points for doing so. Note what you feel.
- Don't do a regular workout at the gym every day. Do enjoy a fun physical activity instead.

PART III

~

DANGERS AND OPPORTUNITIES ON THE ROAD AHEAD: APPLYING THE TOOLS OF CHANGE TO FULCRUM ISSUES

Now let's apply these steps to the specific areas of life that offer great promise and great problems for people who are compulsively driven. I refer to these as fulcrum issues because the way you navigate them will determine how healthy or unhealthy a compulsive you become. I'll point out places where there are opportunities you might otherwise zoom straight past without noticing, and I'll point out dangerous stretches of the road where you could easily lose control of the wheel. At the end of each chapter I'll suggest specific questions, exercises, and approaches to help you steer in these crucial areas.

CHAPTER EIGHT

Body

Mr. Duffy lived a short distance from his body.

—James Joyce, Dubliners

Doris

Doris was a graphic designer who, like James Joyce's character Mr. Duffy, lived a short distance from her body. Well, actually, it was a long distance. It was never consulted when she made her decisions. She worked long hours at her job, where she was constantly in search of perfection. No detail was too small for her attention. No possible problem escaped her scrutiny and foresight. She was constantly on guard that something could go wrong. Since The Evil of Potential Problems never ceased, neither did she. Her colleagues and bosses respected her but thought that her over-the-top controlling actually made her less effective.

She rarely took breaks. She sat on the edge of her chair and leaned over her computer. She was an ergonomic disaster in progress. She was constantly tense, and in the rare moments when she walked away from her computer, you could see the discomfort in how she held herself as she moved.

Still, she was quite likable: friendly, cooperative, a good listener, and affirming. Most of the time. Whenever someone else's work was shoddy and might reflect badly on her, she'd let them know how things were supposed to be done.

Doris was deeply in love with her husband, Kevin, a high school art teacher. She was first attracted to him because he was so relaxed, easy going, and accepting. He was one of the few people who could make her laugh. The two treasured their time together. She tried to be the perfect wife, but she had little interest in sex.

She had put together a beautiful apartment which all their friends complimented her on. But there was a shadow side to the appearance. Everything had to be in order. She didn't just like things looking good, they *had* to look good for her to feel OK. Folding laundry had to be done in a particular way. The cabinets were all organized. While at home she was in perpetual motion cleaning.

Food was the one place she got out of order. Eating was orgasmic for her, the one place she allowed herself any sensual pleasure.

While Doris adored Kevin, she was also secretly angry at him. He didn't get how important it was for her to have things arranged "neatly." He'd leave dishes in the sink, get the cans in the cupboard out of order, and not pick up his clothes. He'd acknowledge he'd made a mess, but didn't share her sense of urgency about cleaning up. But as the perfect wife, she felt she wasn't allowed to express her anger. She coped by stuffing down those feelings, treating herself to rich and sweet foods when she wasn't home.

If you asked her how she was, she'd talk about how much work she'd gotten done. Whether she felt well was of no interest to her. She had no concern for her body. The body has limitations, and she hated limitations. She suffered from mild depression and had difficulty sleeping, but despite her doctor's urging, she wouldn't exercise. Her body was her slave. A hated one at that.

It rebelled, not just with cravings for sweets, but also with injuries, gastrointestinal disorders, and insomnia.

Opportunities

While it's probably true for everyone, it's particularly true for people who are driven that if you learn to listen to your body, it will tell you things you otherwise wouldn't have known about yourself, take you places you otherwise would have missed, ground you in the reality of what's healthy, and provide much-needed pleasure and release.

For instance, you can understand tension in your body not just as a side effect of straining too much, but also as a message that you're damaging your body—a warning signal that lights up. Get sick a lot? Exhausted? Headaches? Back pain? What's your body saying? "Give me a break!"

Another opportunity that a better relationship with your body offers is the capacity to use the body to relax the mind. The mind and body have a reciprocal relationship: the body can follow the mind and the mind can follow the body. Because of this, the body can be used to take the lead in letting go. For instance: if I feel anxious about a deadline, I might tense up physically by raising my shoulders and clenching my jaw; racing thoughts will ensue. Not only is this an inefficient use of my physical energy; it also prevents my best thinking. But if I can relax the body by using progressive muscle relaxation or mindful breathing, the mind slows down so that it can be more effective in meeting that deadline.

Sex, the body's playtime, offers an opportunity to come alive with spontaneity and sensuality. It allows you to let go and lose control for a little while, which is very important for driven people. The French refer to orgasm as *la petite mort*, the little death, the temporary loss or weakening of consciousness—which could be a good thing for compulsives, but it's also one reason they sometimes avoid it.

But sex is only one way that the body can offer pleasure. Massage. The high that comes with a good run. The taste of food and drink. Simply lying down can be savored.

Dangers

The danger for the driven person is that the body becomes a mere vehicle; its pleasures and wisdom are untapped, and it may be treated so badly that it breaks down. Because you have a great capacity to delay gratification and tolerate pain, you may not give your body the attention it needs. Many compulsives, with their predilection for planning, have their center of gravity in their head, not in their body.

Whether you're aware of it or not, if you're overly driven you're probably on high alert physically much of the time: your baseline of arousal is usually high to start, and tension will elevate it even more. Your sympathetic nervous system, which gives you the energy to fight or take flight, is usually in high gear. It's your accelerator, and you've usually got it pressed pretty closely to the floor. Being constantly on, always leaning forward, will eventually take its toll on your body.

Those at the far end of the OCPD spectrum, those whose drive leads them not only to perfection and production but also to anger and hostility, are more likely to develop heart disease. The old theory that Type A folks (people who are competitive, outgoing, ambitious, impatient, and aggressive) have more heart attacks turned out not to be accurate, unless the aggressive element was strongly pronounced and expressed through hostility.[1] So there is a danger here that your compulsiveness earns you a heart attack if you let it make you nasty. But it is not necessarily your fate if your aggressiveness is productive rather than hostile.

The psychological tendency to be rigid, inflexible, and tight are mirrored in the body. You may not allow yourself to breathe deeply, to sleep long enough or well enough, or to rest in any way, because you're always on active duty. What we usually refer to as stress is not just the pressure of your environment, but also your response to that pressure and the stress you put on yourself. If your story and your strategy lead you to be on constant alert, your muscles will become taut, and you are more likely to suffer headaches. You may not give your body the rest it needs to catch up. One woman would not even allow herself the indulgence of going to the bathroom when she was on deadline at work. All of these tendencies can lead to fatigue and burnout.

If you don't allow yourself time to exercise, and you spend all of your time at your desk, you have an increased susceptibility for heart disease, colon cancer, muscle degeneration, foggy thinking, and back problems.[2]

Another danger for compulsives is a neglect of their sensuality and sexuality—the pleasures of the body. While it's true that some people need sex more than others, there is a real danger for those compulsives who think that they can do without it when they really can't. Their sexual needs may rebel and take over the wheel. Affairs ensue. They might find themselves in an intimate but destructive embrace that they hadn't planned on. Others get lost in addiction to pornography. If they've neglected a healthier relationship with their body and real people, they may find themselves glued to alluring images on a computer screen, compulsively clicking, clicking, and clicking, far longer than they meant to, in an unconscious and doomed attempt to develop a better connection to their sensuality.

Then there are those of you who may get that you need sex, but you add it to your list of chores and check it off the second it's done. Or you apply all your perfectionism, compulsive rules, and regulations to it—much to the disappointment and frustration of your partner. Psychologist Nancy MacWilliams once asked a client in a consultation how his sex life with his wife was. His response? "I get the job done."[3]

Some of you may put all your energy into finding or becoming the perfect sexual partner. There is a danger if you are especially attractive or charming that you use these gifts in a compulsive way, neglecting other aspects of yourself to prove your value or to gain security. Or you may use sex or relationships to reassure the frightened child that it won't be abandoned. Exercise and perfecting the body may become compulsive in an attempt to feel more secure.

In all of these dangers, the body becomes a thing, an IT, rather than an aspect of yourself to be loved, honored, and respected.

Doris

Eventually Doris's husband became frustrated with her lack of sexual interest, her need for order, her late nights at work, and her unspoken but deeply felt dismissal of him for not being as meticulous. He insisted that they go to couples therapy together. She balked for months but eventually gave in. When her dissatisfaction with him finally came to the surface in sessions, she held tightly to her position that she was being the reasonable one. Didn't it make sense to have order in the house? Couldn't he see how important these things were to her? Why did he need to have sex more than every few months?

The therapist validated Doris's feeling that he wasn't caring about her but questioned whether that was really the case. Feelings are different from facts. Doris and Kevin came to understand that they had very different needs, and that the needs of each had to be understood and respected. Kevin learned that even though a mess was no big deal in the bigger scheme of the universe, keeping things neat was the best way he could show her his love and help her to be happy. That was important in his universe.

But while Kevin could help, Doris also realized that she wasn't taking care of her own self. She had a moment in which she realized that because she was so focused on making things right outside of her, she wasn't paying attention to her own body. She acknowledged that she didn't feel good about herself, and that she had been fending off dealing with it through work, organizing the home, and an occasional fling with chocolate mousse cheesecake. She allowed herself to feel what would happen if she wasn't perfect, and it was frightening. She knew it wasn't realistic, but she even feared that Kevin would leave her if she didn't keep the house perfectly.

While that session was upsetting, it was also eye-opening for her. She decided to make being kinder to her body her new project. She turned the energy that she usually put into perfection toward feeling better. It wasn't easy, and she had lots of setbacks. She had to sacrifice some perfection. She used the energy and determination that were part of her driven personality to good effect.

Doris had lived her life very deeply in terms of her focus on work and making a beautiful home. But in doing so, she excluded a wider world, which included attention to her body. She had lived only in her mind and never in her body. Part of Doris's work was to broaden her world by going to yoga class regularly, where she became aware of how severe the tension in her body was and learned how to relax it. She didn't just go through the motions. She took the lessons from yoga into her daily life, remembering to check in on her level of physical tension and to exhale deeply. She set limits on how late she would work, and she spoke with Kevin about her fears of leaving things undone at the office. She set aside time each day and weekend to "do nothing." She made a rule for herself to take regular breaks at work and walk for ten minutes.

She and Kevin made it a project to find more pleasurable ways for her to have sex. They took a couples massage workshop together. As she felt better about her body, she enjoyed sex more.

Before having a dessert, she'd ask her body what it really wanted. That often turned out to be release from the perpetual demand to be "on."

Her body ended up being a source of information and pleasure for her, and by paying attention to it she came to release not just physical tension, but emotional tension, too.

Summary

- Treat your body as an ally, not a vehicle or an enemy.
- Learn to recognize from your body when you've entered a compulsive state or are reacting to a disturbing feeling. Notice where you feel tension and urgency: torso leaning forward? Raised shoulders? Clenched jaw, neck, or chest? *Memorize these tense physical sensations so that you recognize when you are afraid of a feeling.*
- Develop the ability to nest or ground lower in the body, in the core closer to your gut.
- Use slow, deep breathing, meditation, yoga, progressive muscle relaxation, or other physical relaxation techniques to learn to recognize where you hold tension in your body, to lower your baseline of physical arousal, and to break patterns of urgency. *Memorize these relaxed physical sensations so that you can call on them and lower physical tension in your everyday life.*
- Learn to use your parasympathetic nervous system, the brakes of your nervous system, to slow things down, both physically and emotionally. Learning to recognize your high arousal and use your brakes to lower it will be essential.
- Check in with your body frequently. Start right now. Take a moment and notice how it's feeling. Are you sitting comfortably? Do you notice any tension? If so, where, specifically? Does that tell you anything? What happens if you try to release the physical tension? See how many times you can do this each day.
- Resist the temptation to make any of these techniques the exclusive focus of your life by becoming compulsive about them. To do so would only change the content of your compulsions without getting at the underlying problem.
- Find healthy ways to honor your sensuality. A single hot bath won't change you, but an ongoing intention to find pleasure in the body can make a difference.

CHAPTER NINE

Time and Money

A man who dares to waste one hour of time has not discovered the value of life.

—Charles Darwin

If more of us valued food and cheer and song above hoarded gold, it would be a merrier world.

—Thorin, speaking of Bilbo in *The Hobbit*

Antoine

Antoine was a forty-year-old college professor with lots of ambition and no time to waste. His students knew him as extremely bright (he'd already published a great deal) but always in a rush. He was known as the Incredible Disappearing Antoine, because he seemed to disappear the second class was over. He was never late for office hours, but he wouldn't stay a second past them either. He'd cut you off midsentence once 4:30 came around. When you did get him to sit down to advise you, you might get the feeling he had better things to do. His timer was always ticking.

Antoine wasn't aware of the way he came across. People experienced him as a little impolite, if not downright rude. He rushed transactions at shops, the doctor's office, and on the phone. He just thought of himself as no-nonsense. When he ran a faculty meeting, you could be sure you'd get out on time. But you might not get a word in.

He practiced short-term serial monogamy, sprinting through relationships quickly with the hope that eventually one of them would understand his need to spend time working. The "candidates," as he called them, noted his urgency. They also noted his frugality. He didn't mind spending money, but he sure as hell wasn't going to waste it. Certain restaurants were deemed too expensive. Not worth it. You could admire that he wasn't ostentatious. His car, clothing, and home furnishings were all very simple. He'd split the bill precisely in honor of gender equality. But his dates didn't appreciate how tightfisted he was. It wasn't unusual for him to question the waiter about the bill.

But his frugality went beyond time and money. He wasn't exactly generous with emotions, compliments, or affection either. He rationalized this tendency to himself by saying that he didn't want to deceive either students or "candidates," so he held back. This mild hoarding pervaded everything he did. He held on to things even when he didn't need to.

At the same time, when he did give, what he gave was rich. His advice to students was always on target. While much of his feedback was negative, he was quite thoughtful when he graded papers. Occasionally, just occasionally, he would say something really nice to someone he was dating. He just refused to waste time, money, or emotion on anything or anyone that wasn't part of his plan. You always knew where he stood. He wouldn't waste words trying to make you feel better.

This might have gone on for a long time had not a group of four graduating seniors decided to play a trick on him. On a drunken whim on graduation day they let the air out of two of the tires on his car and watched in the distance as he went berserk. He was going to miss his flight to a conference, and he didn't want to call someone to fix the tires or call a cab. That would cost too much money. Caught between two of his major issues, he first sat on the ground virtually paralyzed. Then in a fit of anger, he broke his own window.

I've combined time and money in this chapter because the opportunities and dangers are similar: healthy compulsives use their time and money efficiently; unhealthy compulsives feel a need to guard them so preciously that they no longer use them to achieve their goals. If there's one thing that all driven people hate, it's wasting. There's a lot they want to accomplish so they try to make the best possible use of their resources. Nothing is squandered. It was probably someone who was driven who first said "waste not, want not."

While they may be especially careful not to waste time or money, underneath these is a deeper tendency to measure and control carefully that also limits their affection, emotion, and compliments. This tendency can make you either thrifty or stingy, on time or urgent, and genuine or withholding.

Opportunities

People who are driven have the capacity to focus intensely on what's necessary to reach their goals and not waste their resources on less meaningful activities. It seems that they have the genetic disposition toward prudence.[1] Healthy compulsives use their cautiousness and awareness of limitations to help them be productive, reach their aspirations, and avoid impulsive mistakes. Their skills can be helpful in keeping groups on track and reaching their goals.

Healthy compulsives are on time. They measure time in minutes and seconds, not days or hours. They make great timekeepers for groups, formal or informal.

Tempo is a term used in music to describe how quickly the beat occurs, which could be anywhere from 40 beats per minute to 240 beats per minute. Picture the vertical bar on a metronome moving left to right . . . tick . . . tock . . . tick . . . tock, or *ticktockticktock*. Most compulsives have their internal metronome set to a rapid, if not frantic, tempo, trying to save time by being efficient. It can be exhilarating or exhausting.

If you can use your sensitivity to time mindfully, you can choose when to slow down and when to speed up. If you do feel relentless urgency, you can take it as a signal that you're being driven rather than driving consciously. Your sensitivity to time, knowing that time is limited, can help you savor life rather than drive right by it. It encourages you to ask what you're really so urgent about. Where are you driving to? What is it that you really want to accomplish while you still can?

Because they measure money in small denominations, compulsives are more likely to reach their financial goals: buy a car, buy a house, retire, and not go into debt. Their meticulousness, conscientiousness, and integrity make healthy compulsives good treasurers and accountants.

Many healthy compulsives give their time and money generously to good causes—but only if they're certain their gifts won't be wasted. They set a high bar for efficiency, which can serve those causes well.

Dangers

The danger for unhealthy compulsives is that they guard their time and money so vigilantly, rushing and saving, that they don't actually use them to achieve the things that are important to them. But this assumes that they know what the important things are. If they had to become high achieving and self-controlling to reassure themselves that they are loved, or that they won't be controlled by others, they may not have developed a clear sense of their own values, and they live reactively rather than proactively. When compulsives feel that they need to do things to shore up their security or their autonomy, they feel on edge about their resources. They may become rigid and withholding.

Here's how this happens. They may tell themselves a story that goes something like this: they feel they need to prove their value because they feel insecure, and because they feel they need all the time, money, and energy they can muster to prove themselves, they speed up their tempo and hold tightly to whatever they have. Or, as children they feel that their autonomy, individuality, and independence, their very essence, are at risk, and they react by controlling, by clinging to their money and time as symbols of their freedom. In both cases, the danger is that if they use their natural disposition to maintain control, all life becomes infected with a habitual urgency and sense of dire need. The urgency becomes so intense that they speed past the intangibles in life. They become a slave to time and efficiency. They think that by controlling them they are their master, but instead they have become enslaved by them. Efficiency appears to be driving the car, but really fear is.

We tend to become strict and harsh when our motivation is fear rather than desire. Your capacity to be mindful of your limits can be hijacked and placed in the service of defending against fears. So, for instance, if you feel inadequate and that you may be abandoned because of that, you may use your efficiency to try to accomplish goals that you imagine will make others love you. Or, if you fear that others will control you, you may try to maintain your boundaries in order to protect your autonomy. Both situations can lead to an insidious poverty of spirit.

While some compulsives may obsess about and regret past imperfections, many spend most of their time planning the future so that they won't have to regret their mistakes. In both cases the present moment is missed entirely.

Impatience can interfere with relationships. Most people have schedules and tempos that are less dire than yours, and they may experience your impatience as rude and disrespectful. They may feel very low on your list of priorities.

Money promises control and predictability, and as a compulsive, you're in danger of trying to get more money to get more control. More often it delivers stress. As Ralph Waldo Emerson wrote, "Money often costs too much." True, you do need a certain amount of it to be secure and comfortable, but the unhealthy compulsive is at risk of making it their god, of giving it far more importance than is needed. If you aren't clear what's important to you, money may fill the vacuum. It may become an end rather than a means. Think of Ebenezer Scrooge.

There are exceptions to and variations on this theme of hoarding time and money. For example, some unhealthy compulsives can become obsessed with compiling complete sets. For instance, they may develop a compulsion to buy every baseball card ever issued for the Kansas City Royals. Once they start collecting it's hard to stop. Their need for completion may override their frugal tendency.

In some instances collecting can turn to hoarding. Hoarding occurs when people excessively save items that others view as worthless. They end up with clutter that disrupts their ability to use their living or work spaces. Both people with OCD and OCPD can be inclined to hoard, though the worse cases are more characteristic of people with OCD. Compulsives are likely to collect and organize, but less likely to stack the living room with decades of newspapers.

Antoine

Antoine knew he had gone over the edge when he broke his own car window, and that he should probably do something about it. It was like Ebenezer Scrooge's wakeup nightmare. But the idea of going to therapy pushed his buttons: it costs time and money. It requires a certain amount of vulnerability. Yet he had known for a while that things weren't right with him. He suspected there was some reason, not a good one, that he went through dating "candidates" so quickly. Maybe there was even a reason the students had played the prank on him. But most of all he wasn't happy. Antoine didn't buy into the American assumption that we should all be happy all the time. Still, almost never being happy didn't seem right either. It was worth a try.

Once we began therapy, I had to relieve Antoine of his sense that he needed to keep track of time in the session. He had been keeping his eye on the clock to see how much time we had left. "That's my job," I told him. It was hard on him at first to let go. It felt out of control. He spoke to me about his fears that therapy would control him by making him slow down too much.

When Antoine told me about the times when he got into arguments about money, I got him to check in with his body to see what he experienced there as he told me about them. He noticed a visceral reaction, as if having to fend off an attack on his body, as if someone were going to take something out of him. We stayed with this feeling of something being taken from him, and he recalled when he felt that his parents tried to take his plans away from him.

At first he recalled their intense disapproval when he said he wanted to come to New York for college. But that was only the most recent episode in a long history of feeling controlled. His mother was a very insecure woman who needed Antoine's constant presence. But she also rejected him when he didn't do what she wanted him to do. His natural curiosity and desire to explore felt stolen. When they did start to allow him some freedom, it was always time-limited. "OK. You can go out for a bike ride for twenty minutes, but you'd better be back on time." He felt pressed to make the best of his time away from them. He'd always been an active and energetic child, sprinting from one activity to another, and his parents' restrictions only increased his habitual tempo.

He wanted to play down the money issue with me. "Money doesn't really mean a lot to me. It's just a means to an end."

"What's the end?"

"Well, I can do things."

"Like what?"

"I don't know. Like take trips. Travel."

"When was the last time you travelled, other than visiting your parents? We both know how much you enjoyed that."

"Are you trying to make me have fun?"

"Heaven forbid."

He got my point. Money wasn't about money. It was about being able to do what he wanted. But he had lost track of what he wanted. As he faced his fears of not having enough, he realized that his concern about money was costing him too much emotionally. That concern for money would never go away completely. Life is expensive, and academics don't get paid a lot. But our work did take enough of the intensity out of his frugality that he didn't need to get out a calculator on a date any more. He began to travel for pleasure, not just conferences.

Antoine also had to ask similar questions about time. He had to sort out when he was rushing out of habit, and when there was something he really wanted or needed to do. He monitored his frustration when he was delayed and tried to breathe through it rather than break windows. He learned to recognize when he felt urgency, and to question where he really wanted to go.

Antoine's biggest challenge was to stay with feelings long enough to let them register and eventually pass through him. While he hadn't experienced trauma or deprivation, he still had feelings of anger, sadness, and fear that he had avoided by focusing on achievement most of his life.

He continued to conduct research, but he focused more on his original interests than on publishing out of a fear that he would perish. He also started to enjoy his discussions with students, remembering the ideas that had brought him into his field in the first place. He realized that he had been unnecessarily withholding praise for them and began to give compliments whenever he could do so honestly.

In regard to other people, he had to ask himself whether they were really taking his autonomy away from him, or whether he was just being overly vigilant about it. What did he really need his autonomy for? He met and dated a woman who was actually more highly strung than he was. He was able to see his own foibles more clearly by observing hers. She had her own goals, and he didn't feel that she threatened his autonomy. Ironically, he was the one that began suggesting a slower pace for the two of them.

Summary

- Identify whether you tend to hold too tightly to time, money, autonomy, or anything else. Get to know the feeling—emotional and physical—that comes with holding on. Recognize it as often as you can.
- Allow yourself to feel what would happen if you did slow down or spend money. What are your fears? Could you tolerate the consequences?
- Practice identifying your tempo. On a scale of one to ten, how fast are you going right now? How fast do you go on average?
- Practice taking off your watch or not checking the time on your phone. Each time you feel the urge to look at the time, ask: What is my rush? Where are I am going?
- Explore how time has figured into your story, and the strategy you've used to deal with that story.
  - What do you believe you need to accomplish and how soon?
  - What feeling do you want to run away from?
  - Does being rushed fit in with your aspirations?
  - Is there a particular voice or character in your head that rushes you?
- Use delays as opportunities to breathe deeply and regain contact with your body. Every time you're forced to wait, drop any physical tension, pay attention to your breathing, and reaffirm what's most important to you. Count the times you can do this each day.

- Use delays as an opportunity to come face to face with your fear of not achieving enough. That in itself may be worth slowing down for.
- Looking back over the past week, identify as many episodes as you can in which you savored the present moment rather than planned the future or regretted the past.
- Notice if you fear people taking away your time, money, or autonomy.
- Ask if your goals might be unrealistic, setting you up for a constant sense of falling behind.
- Make slowing down physically and mentally a priority that overrides productivity. If you can't achieve something without being rushed, maybe you shouldn't be doing it.
- Notice what you feel when money is asked of you.
- Clarify what you want money for. How much do you need?
- Quit focusing on the content (the money or time) and focus instead on your physical and emotional experience. Are you clinging or letting go?

CHAPTER TEN

Work and Career

I am doomed to an eternity of compulsive work. No set goal achieved satisfies. Success only breeds a new goal. The golden apple devoured has seeds. It is endless.

—Bette Davis

This is the real secret of life—to be completely engaged with what you are doing in the here and now. And instead of calling it work, realize it is play.

—Alan Watts

Jill

Jill, a thirty-four-year-old magazine editor, had come from a family in a small midwestern town that was bound to skew compulsive tendencies in an unhealthy direction. Her father was a quite severe minister who focused more on God's wrath than on His love and forgiveness. Her mother was a germ-phobic stay-at-home mom with OCD. Her religion was cleaning.

Jill didn't believe in her father's religion, but she did share his intensity. She didn't inherit her mother's OCD genes, but she was the victim of her vehement insistence on cleanliness. The takeaway message from her parents was that there was always some lurking evil that needed to be completely eradicated, and you should never rest until it was. But it never was.

The middle of three children, Jill was emotional and passionate, but there was little room for her feelings in the home, so she ended up spending most of her time alone. She wasn't rebellious, but she couldn't sign on to the family religions either.

In church she'd sit through her father's sermons uncomfortably, wondering if he was talking to her. She watched him discipline her older brother physically and severely for not being home in time for dinner, not studying enough, or not doing his chores. She watched her younger sister perpetually trying to please her parents in any way she could. Both made her nervous: one by getting in trouble for not doing enough, the other by losing herself by doing too much.

She dealt with her situation partly by writing. In private she filled journal after journal, at first with simple stories, and as she grew older with more sophisticated fiction and reams of poetry. In public she tried to express herself in a way that was acceptable to her parents. She devoured grammatical rules in English class, pleasing the teacher to no end. By the time she finished high school, she had won several awards for her writing and was able go away to an excellent college on a scholarship. She did well there, but no one graduates with a job writing fiction and poetry. Instead she got a job as a copy editor at a magazine.

At first it was just a job she was happy to have to support herself while she worked on her own writing. But something kicked in once she started. She loved finding mistakes. She loved making corrections. It was as if she got a small hit of endorphins each time she did. On the one hand editing came naturally to her. On the other hand, doing it also silenced, albeit temporarily, the nagging sense that she was supposed to be doing something that cleaned things up. Her attention to detail and her strong work ethic helped her move up the ranks in the publishing firm where she worked. She found it immensely satisfying to complete projects, and over time it seemed that finishing became more gratifying than the editing itself. But the satisfaction was short-lived. What was next? Eventually each project just seemed like something else to finish.

Her attention to work was causing other problems too. She worked on her own writing less and less and spent more and more time at the office. She kept telling herself she'd get back to her writing. Her partner, Mary, objected to her late (and early) hours, and, even more, she objected to Jill's neglect of her creative side. That was part of what she loved about her. But Jill was having a really hard time tearing herself away from the office and the identity she took on there. She tried to spend more time outside of work, but she felt very anxious that she was dropping the ball. "Good enough" was not in her vocabulary.

Her strengths almost led to her downfall. At a time when the standards of magazine writing were changing drastically, she remained insistent on old style proper grammar. Or at least she tried to. She became so persnickety about it that her relations with her colleagues and writers began to suffer. As she began to feel more insecure, she used the same strategy she always had: work harder. She stayed later to make sure her edits were correct, justified, and perfect. Rather than confront her feelings of insecurity directly, she simply worked more and fought more. Her job and her relationship were both in jeopardy. She would not have been able to articulate this, but her Inner Preacher had taken over.

Opportunities

Healthy compulsives use their natural inclination to strive to provide for themselves or their families, to be productive and creative, and to complete projects others might only dream about. It can help them to get where they want to go.

But the greater opportunities are intrinsic. I probably don't need to tell you that finishing high-quality work can be enormously fulfilling. It satisfies one of our deepest motivations,[1] which, if denied, can lead to depression.[2] Especially for someone who's driven, it gratifies a deep compelling urge. But it's important to remember that work is even more satisfying when you savor the process, not just the result. Whether that's relishing the banishment of a superfluous comma, appreciating the feel of a good throw to first base, or genuinely enjoying the socializing before a big sale, savoring the moment is more satisfying, improves work performance, and prevents burnout.

Dangers

But because people who are driven tend to lean into the future and not the present, they often miss opportunities to savor their work. It may become habitual drudgery rather than satisfying challenge. Despite being the source of some of our most profound satisfaction, work has its dangers—especially for people who are driven. Let me count the ways.

Addiction: When You Can't Stop Working

It's obvious that people who are compulsive often work too much. What's not so obvious is that work can be seriously and debilitatingly addictive.[3] Addiction occurs not just with substances but also with behaviors. These are known as process addictions.[4] Here are some indications that you may be addicted:

- Salience: the activity becomes the most important thing in your life.
- Mood modification: doing the activity makes you feel better at first.
- Tolerance: you need to spend more time doing the activity to get the high.
- Withdrawal symptoms: you feel uncomfortable when you're not doing the activity.
- Conflict: a battle evolves within yourself or with people around you about how much time you spend in the activity.
- Relapse: you try to stop the activity but fail.

Take this test to see whether you might have a work addiction.

The Bergen Work Addiction Scale (BWAS)[5]
Ask yourself whether you do the following: (1) = Never, (2) = Rarely, (3) = Sometimes, (4) = Often, and (5) = Always.

- You think of how you can free up more time to work.
- You spend much more time working than initially intended.
- You work in order to reduce feelings of guilt, anxiety, helplessness, and depression.
- You have been told by others to cut down on work without listening to them.

- You become stressed if you are prohibited from working.
- You deprioritize hobbies, leisure activities, and exercise because of your work.
- You work so much that it has negatively influenced your health.

If you responded "often" or "always" on at least four of the seven items, you may be a workaholic.

The research regarding work addiction is still emerging. It's not the kind of calamity that has foundations clamoring to fund it. While research has revealed the dangers of work addiction,[6] the biological mechanisms involved have not been defined clearly. But there is increasing evidence that people who have a strong sense of intrinsic motivation, which is highly characteristic of the driven personality, do so because they experience a greater than normal burst of dopamine when they are engaged in a satisfying challenge.[7]

It makes intuitive sense that completing a project would stimulate your natural reward system, giving you a hit of endorphins or opioids with each task you complete. Do your own research. Note how you feel the next time you check something off your list and compare it to the times when you weren't able to work for some reason. See whether it feels like there's something chemically pleasant going on inside your brain each time you accomplish something, and whether it could be addictive for you.

This is not to say that it's only neurochemical. As with other behavioral addictions such as exercise addiction, internet addiction, or sex addiction, behavior starts for purely psychological reasons and then incites a biological cycle that becomes even harder to break. There is a reason that your cravings to work feel incredibly intense.

People who are driven are particularly vulnerable to becoming addicted to the use of computers, tablets, mobile phones, and the internet. Because you're capable of shutting everything else out and focusing intently, and because you feel the need to be thorough, without realizing it you may become more attached to devices than to people or other sources of gratification. You may think that you're doing something for your own sake, but instead you've entered a trance and gotten sucked into something you hadn't intended to. Your never-ending quest for completion and solutions may lead you to check out every web page on the internet that has information about the most efficient way to repair that crack in the wall that's been driving you crazy. Because you may intensely seek answers or solutions, the internet can grab your attention and never let it go. "Just one more click and I'll be finished."

Perfectionism: When Your Standards Create Harmful Pressure

It's not just how much you work; it's also how you work that affects your quality of life. If you're perfectionistic, and the quality of your work becomes the basis for your identity, it's more likely that tension and anxiety will infect your vocation. You may become very anxious if you feel that you aren't "performing" perfectly; it becomes a haunting question in the back of your mind as to whether your work, and therefore you, are good enough.

This often happens when productivity is hijacked to prove personal worth. The stakes skyrocket. This makes it much harder to savor work because it's motivated by fear, not by love. This may also lead you to contaminate your work with urgency. If you're in a rush to complete it and cross it off your list, it will be harder to enjoy. If you feel that someone is getting in the way of you accomplishing your work tasks, it will cause interpersonal conflict.

Tension and perfectionism can lead to unnecessary levels of grasping. I often demonstrate this to patients with a tissue box. Holding the box in one hand I crush it with tension. Then I simply hold the box lightly without crushing it. No need to crush the box to hold it. Whatever your task, whatever you need to hold on to, hold it lightly, not tightly. When you do need to work intensely, you can work from a place of desire rather than fear.

If you're too critical of your work, and don't appreciate what you have accomplished or the process of accomplishing it, you will continue to feel unsatisfied and intensify the cycle of work addiction.

A related problem and a form of perfectionism that many compulsives experience is the need to fix and complete. While this can help you follow through, some issues can't be fixed, and some projects can't be completed. If you don't learn to let go, you may end up feeling uneasy with mental clutter of unresolved issues. You may end up putting off activities that would balance you more until those issues are resolved.

Burnout: When Working Too Hard Leads to Diminishing Returns

Another danger from an emphasis on work and perfectionism is burnout.[8] The typical cause of burnout for compulsives is that they set up expectations that are beyond their capability. Burnout can result from a conflict between what you want to do or think you should do, and what's actually possible—for instance, insisting that you impress and please everyone you work for and with, and that you produce perfectly no matter what the external obstacles are. People who are driven often refuse to take into consideration that the situation they are working in, or the people they are working with, won't allow them to be as productive as they would like to be. They often feel that they should be able to override any obstacles and achieve perfection. As one client told me, "impossible" just wasn't in his vocabulary.

Burnout manifests in cynicism, fatigue, irritability, lack of satisfaction, use of addictions to feel better, over- or undersleeping, over- or undereating, and physical complaints. It tends to develop slowly, and you may not be aware of it until you are deeply in its clutches.

Distraction and Avoidance: Hidden Motivations for Working Too Much

Another danger with work is that you could use it to mask psychological issues that need to be dealt with directly but have been too distressing to face. Work may become a form of self-medication,[9] trying to make yourself feel better without addressing the real problem of insecurity, anger, depression, or emptiness. Working late or long hours can be enlisted as a passive-aggressive way of expressing anger at a partner who wants more from you—seemingly with the justification of providing for the family.

For some, working hard may be an overcompensation for an unacknowledged and forbidden desire to slow down or be more playful or messy, an effort to silence a part of the personality that needs to have some expression. Many clients have told me that they're afraid that if they slow down at all they'll never get up and work again. You may be afraid that the child part of you (or the aging part of you) will take over and get you in trouble.

For others, overworking may be an effort to control the uncontrollable world outside of them, trying to distract from feeling vulnerable to the realities of the world. If you've been the victim of trauma or catastrophe, taking on heroic challenges may seem to reassure that you can control the uncontrollable. Here again, work itself might not be an issue, but too much of it or an emphasis on it may keep you from facing emotional issues that need to be addressed directly to get to the healthy side of compulsive.

Neglect: Excluding Other Parts of Life

Even if you're not actually addicted to work, there is still a danger that working too much could lead to the neglect of other important areas of your life such as relationships, rest, leisure, and health. Neglecting these makes you vulnerable to both physical and mental health issues. I'll say more about the value of rest and relationships in the next two chapters.

If you're too focused on tangible progress at your workplace, you may neglect the intangibles, such as telling others what you appreciate about them and their work.

Caveats

But let's also be realistic. Most of us do need to work, and keeping our job is dependent on delivering acceptable work on time. It is true that there is usually external pressure to achieve—often quite demanding pressure. Still, there is a difference between external and internal pressure, and creating more internal pressure to achieve will magnify the external pressure. Those with Type A personality, for instance, were found to react to stress with more psychological strain than those with Type B personality.[10]

Many people fear that without using the proverbial stick (as opposed to the carrot) to prod themselves, they will not only fail at their job, they will also end up desolate on skid row. Among the driven people I've known, I've never seen it happen. Prodding with the stick just creates tension that makes it harder to succeed. While you usually can't control the amount of external pressure at your job, you can control how much internal pressure you add.

If you have a job that actually makes it hard for you to complete work that you feel has value, this will be an especially difficult area for you. Barring finding another job, you may need to have other outlets for your creativity and drive to produce.

Jill

Once things came to a head at her job and with her partner, Jill decided to seek help. She wasn't happy with her life either. As we began exploring her story, it became clear that Jill had never dealt with her feelings about her parents' discipline. Understandably, she had tried to simply focus her attention on psychic survival until she could get out of the house. She began to see that while she disagreed with both of her parents about what was important, she had actually adopted the same adamancy about values. In effect she had become like them, even though she valued different things. She thought she had left them behind when she moved away, but they had followed her to the big city in a big way. She had struck a compromise when she developed her strategy: she could disagree with her parents, but only if she worked just as hard as they did; she could leave their values behind only if she was just as rigid about her own values.

The strategy worked well for a while. But eventually it failed because it didn't address the real problem. She was never convinced that she was OK. She kept trying to prove it.

Jill set an intention to make serious changes. She looked honestly at herself to see whether she needed to prove herself with work. Yes, she had her quirks, and over the last few years she had become difficult to be around, but in the end she concluded she was basically good, and she didn't have to prove her goodness to herself. It meant facing fears of damnation and rejection, and taking chances of being found guilty. It felt strange and scary, but she set strict limits on how late she worked. She learned to think in terms of "good enough."

This conversation with herself was hard fought, and the issue will always need her conscious attention so that she doesn't slip back into the feelings of not being adequate.

We worked to develop empathy for the child raised in a world that felt totally foreign to her. None of it had made sense to her, and she had

had to find some way to get through it until she could get out. Not that she was so aware of it when it was happening, but tenderness toward herself was forbidden by her father's discipline. The nervous sense that there was always something dangerous around put her constantly on guard.

She knew she needed to let go of her reactions to her past, to let go of her need to assure herself that she was good. She had been fighting for self-assurance in a battle disguised in skirmishes over commas and semicolons. No one had told Jill to stay late at work doing this. As is characteristic of people with work addiction, she worked far more than was necessary. But just stopping the battle only left her empty. She also needed something meaningful to hold onto.

The part of her that was insecure had been stealing time and energy from the part that was driven to creative self-expression. Over time she took the energy that had gone into correcting other people's writing and returned it to her own writing. She went to bed at a decent hour and got up early to write before she went to work. She began writing poetry again—fierce poetry that didn't kowtow to her parents or an English teacher. She put the creative part back in the driver's seat and put the critical part in the backseat, where she could call on it when she needed it.

As she became less identified with editing, it took less energy. She could still get that good feeling when she caught something wrong and made it right. But it was no longer a matter of life and death. She also realized that it was much easier to edit other people than to take the chance of writing her own poems and short stories. Work had also served the function of avoiding her fears about her own abilities.

Her relationship with Mary began to revive. She realized that her intense devotion to work had allowed her to avoid difficult conversations she'd been dreading. Those went more smoothly than she expected: she had been projecting her own judgmental voice into Mary, imagining Mary was angrier at her then she really was.

These concrete changes were manifestation of a deeper transformation that took place over time. As she came to understand her life story and the strategy she had adapted, internal relationships shifted. She mapped out the characters who had peopled it: the passionate child, the frightened child, and the Preacher, the hardworking, rulebound part that had seemed to protect her from her family, but had really only replicated it. A calmer, more mature part of her that could listen to all of the other parts emerged to help her make more balanced decisions. This part helped her pursue goals that were more natural and authentic for her.

Summary

- Make an honest appraisal as to whether you have a work addiction. Remember that denial and rationalization are the two favorite defenses of people with addictions. If you are addicted, make a plan with specific intentions to pull back. Prepare yourself for withdrawal symptoms. Find the core of what you need from work and honor that. Let others know that you are trying to change.
- Make an honest appraisal as to whether you're burned out. If you are, devise a plan to pull back. You may need help from a professional, support group, or very committed friends to break the cycle and find a way out.
- Make self-care a priority: allow time to eat well, sleep, exercise, and relax.
- Determine where to draw the line as to when you work too much. Take into consideration not just the hours you work, but also what work time excludes, how much time it allows you to spend on relationships and other activities. Draw a pie chart and see what the balance looks like.
- When you are working, identify as many things as you can that you like about it. Give yourself more points for appreciating the process, not just the end product.
- But also do give yourself credit for your accomplishments.
- Set clear boundaries so that technology doesn't take over your steering wheel. The next time you're at a computer or using a phone or tablet, ask yourself, "Who's in control here now?"
- When you find yourself caught in a work binge, ask: "What inner character is driving me now?"
- Set a goal to learn to tolerate imperfections and mistakes. Welcome them as opportunities to be more human and to work on the really important issues—your emotional health.

- Examine your motivation for working so hard: Is it fear or desire? Avoidance or approach?
- Notice if there are emotions (or relationships) that you are trying to avoid by working.
- Divest and expand. Put your productive and creative energies into projects other than your job. That may not be easy at first.
- Stop working mentally on projects and issues that are unresolved. Take time regularly to see if there are issues that feel unsettled for you and release them.

~

CHAPTER ELEVEN

People, Partners, and Parenting

Immature love says: "I love you because I need you." Mature love says "I need you because I love you."

—Erich Fromm

Ted

Ted was an exceedingly bright child. He loved puzzles. He loved solving problems. He had an intellectual curiosity that led him to read books most kids couldn't be bothered with at his age. He was driven in his quiet way.

Many driven people become unhealthy compulsives when their parents rigidly emphasize doing things the "right" way. Ted's parents had a slightly different focus: They were anxious to fit in, and they emphasized not what they believed was the moral course of action, but rather what other people thought. They used a shame-based approach: "If you don't play baseball, the other kids will tease you." "If you wear that shirt, the teachers won't respect you." "If you read too much, they'll think you think you're better than they are." His parents didn't understand that Ted was driven to learn and accomplish things irrespective of what others thought. He felt like a different breed, always being watched for possible violations of a code he didn't get. It distracted him from what he really wanted to do. He hated it, but he also didn't want to be made fun of by his peers.

There were some reasons for his parents' concerns, but the message was so strong that it overwhelmed Ted's natural feelings for people. The fear that he would be judged and perhaps controlled by others contaminated the enjoyment he would have otherwise had. The way they described the world, relationships seemed limiting, oppressing, and suffocating. But like any human being, he couldn't just write people off completely. It set up an internal conflict between the part of him that wanted to be loved rather than shamed, and the part that wanted to be authentic and creative.

The conflict became apparent in ninth grade, when he had an experience that confirmed his fears about people. For a few years he had often played the fantasy game Dungeons and Dragons with two friends. He enjoyed spending time with them and loved sharing the challenges the games offered. He had a chance to use his intelligence and creativity. But when his friends started experimenting with pot and acid, they put heavy pressure on Ted to do the same. He tried pot but didn't like the experience. It made him feel groggy, and he stopped spending time with them. After that they ridiculed him every chance they had at school.

Without realizing it, Ted arrived at a compromise: he did whatever he was supposed to do so that people would think he was a good person, but he didn't get close enough that they would have control over him. This way he wouldn't be shamed by others, but he also wouldn't lose himself. Or such was the unconscious strategy. He spent time with other students at school, but went home alone to study or work on the articles he wrote for the school paper. He was friendly enough, but he didn't form the close bonds that most kids long for in school. In college he wrote for the school paper where he had good collegial relationships and was respected for his hard work and critical thinking. He had some sexual relationships but wouldn't commit to anything deeper. He was too busy studying.

But the need for love doesn't go away. It just waits for a moment when it seems safe to come out.

People

The opportunities and dangers for driven people in relationships are particularly tricky and the stakes are very high. Qualities that are typical of healthy compulsives, such as being loyal, committed, consistent, reliable, and trustworthy, help them form and sustain fulfilling and enriching relationships. Other characteristics that can be typical of less healthy compulsives, such as being righteous, judgmental, nagging, hostile, and impatient, lead to deeply conflicted relationships, destroy them, or prevent them from happening in the first place.[1]

The irony of compulsives' fraught relationships is that if you ask them why they insist so staunchly on their rules, most of them would say that the rules are needed to help or protect people. Remembering this original intention, and finding a way to honor it, will help you to be a healthier compulsive. But this isn't a simple proposition. Over time you may have wired yourself so that your energy flows more naturally to achievement and judgment than toward alliance and community, and overriding that may be difficult at first. But it is possible, and the rewards are well worth it.

First we'll look at the opportunities and dangers of relationships in general for people who are driven. Then we'll look at the particular ways these issues show up between partners, and then between parents and children. We'll follow Ted's story throughout and conclude the chapter with suggestions as to how people who are driven can navigate and enjoy relationships.

Opportunities

I wrote earlier that the road to becoming a healthier compulsive returns to your deepest urges so that you can find a more conscious and fulfilling way of responding to them. Perhaps two of the greatest opportunities and deepest urges in life are to love and to be loved. Our capacity for bonding is part of what has helped the human race to flourish. The need for it is deeply embedded in our nature, and Nature has seen to it that the rewards for bonding are great: the relief of sharing emotional burdens, the delight of a friend's smile or laughter, the gratification of helping someone in need, savoring food or good music together, knowing there are others you can count on in times of need, and the excitement and learning that comes with exploring ideas with others. As a Harvard University longitudinal study reports, good relationships correlate with longer, happier, and healthier lives.[2]

Dangers

If these benefits seem frivolous to you, it's probably because somewhere along the way love seemed either too limiting or too scary, and you traded the desire for love for the desire for respect. It felt like the best compromise possible. Achievement, and the respect that came with it, probably seemed much more under your control. But while respect may be a form of love, there are deeper, more compelling possibilities.

While some people need relationships more than others, in most cases if relationships are low on your list of priorities it's because they were pushed down, not because that need wasn't there to start. It's universal. But this need for connection is a little different for people who are driven. In addition to urges to connect, they also have powerful urges to accomplish that need to be recognized along with the need to connect. Conflicts often arise between the two.

Unhealthy compulsives tend to focus more on what researchers call agency (focus on oneself and achieving autonomy) to the exclusion of communion (focus on others and forming connections).[3] There are benefits to agency such as independence, self-reliance, being able to make yourself happy, and pursuing your own goals. There are also benefits to communion, such as social support, feedback, empathy, and shared pleasures. The research tells us that focusing on either agency or communion to the extent that it excludes the other leads us to become unhealthy, physically and emotionally. If you focus too much on agency, you miss the opportunities of relationship, and vice versa.

One of the many ways that compulsives control is to manage distance in relationships. In addition to managing distance to protect their projects, they also manage it to protect their autonomy. Many fear that getting too close to someone would require them to sacrifice their independence, along with their goals. Many felt when they were young that they had to restrain and constrict themselves to be loved in their family.

They felt that such narrowing of their personality would keep them from being themselves and achieving what they felt compelled to.

This is a fundamental conflict for many people who are driven: relationships are important to them, but they also have a sense of purpose that they fear relationships will preclude. The danger is that you err on the side of independence and agency in order to protect your autonomy, and you then miss out on the advantages of close relationships and communion.

Some compulsives do what they think other people want them to do, but then feel anger and resentment about not being able to be more authentic. Some simply avoid relationships completely. Others elect for a compromise: they enter into relationships but try not to become too deeply attached.

Still, compulsives can have very high standards for behavior in relationships: they respond to communication, they show up on time. They always do what's expected of them, but with the expectation that others will be as dependable as they are. They may have difficulty forgiving others for not behaving the same way. But not everyone else signs on to those standards.

You might feel like people who aren't driven are like muggles, the "normals" in the Harry Potter mythology who don't have the gift of magic (or being driven) and can't see its possibilities. But this assumes compulsives are better than "normals." Differences aren't all bad. They make our world a richer place. Without "normals," there would be little of the spontaneity and flexibility they bring to our world. People who are more casual do have their role. They can be more easygoing, funny, relaxing, accepting, and creative. A world full of compulsive people would be dreary and relentless.

But you may have a hard time with "normals." Because they tend to be more spontaneous and less controlled, they get in the way of one of your basic strategies: prediction. That's the wonderful and distressful thing about people. You can't control them. People who are driven run into danger when they need others to follow their rules and be predictable, and they may exert excessive control to get others to comply. This is not a good way to win friends and influence people. Rather it leads to a sanctimonious attitude, loss of relationships, and isolation. Forcibly trying to reform others rarely works anyway.

People may perceive your determination to make things better differently from the way you intend it. Even if you don't apply your personal standards to other people, they may assume you do, and feel that you're always looking down your nose at them. This could easily be the case if you aren't very communicative. What may feel to you like well-intended efforts to help may be experienced by others as mean-spirited criticism, control, or hostility.[4]

This can show up in the workplace. Busting people's chops for even minor infractions seems justified to people who are driven in order for things to run better. But in the long term it erodes the quality of those relationships and destroys any leverage you may have to get them to sign on to higher standards. Since compulsives live to solve problems, they may not notice that their responses are grating, and they tend not to voice affirmation when others have worked hard.

Communities such as faith groups, sports teams, volunteer organizations, or professional societies offer a place for driven people to socialize and contribute their skills in a meaningful way. But communities move slowly, and they require great patience of people who need to be efficient. Still, the rewards of service can be very fulfilling, and the social benefits they could derive from a social network may not be obvious to compulsives.

Perhaps the ugliest danger for compulsives in regard to people is that others cease to be people: they become either vehicles to move projects forward, or simply objects that block the way. While compulsive people may be painfully lonely underneath, they may self-medicate with productivity and remain unaware of their deeper needs for connection.

Finally, relationships engender emotion, and many compulsives feel much safer avoiding emotions other than anger. Sadness, longing, and anxiety often come with relationships, but they come with the territory of a broadened approach to life and being a healthier compulsive.

Ted Starts His Family

Eight years later Ted has passed the bar and is working for a law firm. His colleagues have managed to rope the well-documented party pooper into having a few drinks. When he sees Dana sitting at the bar, he becomes transfixed. It wasn't just that she was pretty; it was that she was so lively, cheerful, and animated. Even while sitting she danced. He couldn't take his eyes off her, but he wasn't skilled at pickup lines. It was only pure luck that he managed to get a seat next to her at the bar. She started the conversation. She smiled. She laughed. A lot. She was easy to talk to. He felt no judgment from her. She was everything he didn't allow himself to be. She asked if he'd take her to a jazz club sometime and he jumped at the possibility. She made him feel like no one ever had, and he wasn't going to miss this opportunity to feel better.

It was the moment when his need for love finally felt that it was safe to come out.

Dana saw Ted as very stable, and after a string of unstable men in her life, this was a welcome quality. Yes, he was a little tight, but he'd loosen up with time. So she thought.

They married, bought the house, had the kids, and, looking back over the last fifteen years, it felt to Dana as if Ted had missed the whole thing. He'd been at work the whole time. Even when he wasn't literally at work, he was at work in his head. Relationships were confusing to him, and work was satisfying and simpler. Without realizing it, he slowly drifted into a work addiction. Try as he might, he just couldn't focus on other things. When their daughter and son began to struggle with psychological and behavioral issues, he left it to Dana to handle them. He told himself she was better at that kind of thing.

They lived in the same house but existed miles apart from each other emotionally. He couldn't understand how she could just sit around and watch television. He had disdain for her women's group. He hated that she laughed so much. All the things that originally attracted him to her now drove him crazy. Didn't she understand that there were serious problems to be solved? How could she move so slowly all the time? He had long ago taken over the accounting because he didn't trust her to do it correctly. He came to experience her as a nag because she tried to get him to spend more time with the family. He was angry at her, but he wasn't direct about it. He expressed it passively, with distance.

She couldn't understand how he could actually enjoy reading those legal documents he spent so much time buried in. He seemed to love them more than her. Why did he have to be in such a rush all the time? When they went out with friends, he seemed bored and impatient. Even rude at times. This was not what she had imagined.

He imagined that she wanted to control him, and she imagined that he was judging her. They were both right, and they were both wrong.

By this point Ted knew that things were way off in their marriage, but he was afraid that if he tried to explore it with her things would only get worse. She might decide that one of them had fallen out of love and so they should divorce. Better to avoid it. Or so he rationalized his behavior to himself. It became a very powerful motivator to stay late at work. He didn't like a lot of what she did, but he hated change even more. Besides, divorce was shameful and he still cared more about what other people thought than about how he felt.

The truth was it was himself he was avoiding talking to. He didn't want to acknowledge his deep discontent, his work addiction, and his failing marriage. He loved the rush of work, solving legal problems, and the approbation and money that came with it. Socializing paled in comparison. But, had he been honest with himself, it also seemed that the work never let up, and even though he enjoyed some of it, it was beginning to take a toll on him. What had been interesting was becoming mechanical—like someone addicted to drugs who now uses them just not to feel bad, rather than using them to feel good, Ted used work to distract himself from the real problems of deep dissatisfaction and a failing marriage rather than to take pleasure in solving intellectual problems. He was aware of feeling urgency about work matters, but he blocked out the urgency about his emotions and relationships that were the real issues.

One night, after a particularly bad fight with Dana over the phone about working late, he went out for an innocent drink with the new associate. Taking the edge off turned to taking clothes off and it turned less than innocent. It was, in a way, a replay of his first night with Dana: he discovered someone who left him feeling free to be himself and he couldn't pass up the opportunity. It lasted only eight hours, but those were a very destructive eight hours. He tried to cover it up, but it was so out of character that Dana knew something had happened and he had to confess. It was a shock to both of them.

Partners

For better or worse, compulsives tend not to partner with compulsives. They usually tend to be drawn to someone who can bring feeling and spontaneity into their life. This feels wonderful at first and crazy making down the line. Expecting someone to live things out for you that you don't live yourself is a dangerous proposition. It also means that neither partner grows.

Too often compulsives set up a division of labor in their intimate relationships: "I'll be reasonable and careful and productive, and you live out all my wild stuff." This may work for a while, but it causes problems after the thrill has worn off and you hate everything you loved about them at the start: their relaxed pace, more easygoing standards, and more accepting attitude. These differences are battled out in small skirmishes about the toothpaste cap that's left off, the dishwasher that's not loaded efficiently, and the light that was left on for thirty seconds too long. But they're all really about the larger war over whether it's better to be careful or casual.

Because compulsives often feel adamantly that they're right, and that they *should* fight for what's right as a matter of principle, they have a difficult time hearing their partner and compromising. Being right may feel more important than maintaining a good relationship.

While unhealthy compulsives can become openly hostile, most compulsives have difficulty expressing their anger directly, and, without realizing it, they often resort to passive-aggressive behavior. It seems to them to be the best way to handle the situation, quietly punishing the other person for what they've done wrong, with the hope that they'll realize the error of their ways.

When a driven person does partner with another driven person, it tends to either amplify the possible benefits or ensure the potential catastrophes that the style invites; they may support each other in both productivity and avoidance, adapting brilliantly to the outer world but not at all to their inner worlds. What might seem absolutely crazy to your everyday nondriven person begins to seem perfectly normal in the bubble of the compulsive world they create together. In a partnership like this all the nuances and pleasures of life become sacrificed to the gods of productivity, perfection, and efficiency.

Ted Struggles with His Kids

Ted loved his kids, but he was absolutely baffled by them. They just weren't reasonable. They seemed so foreign. How could these be his kids? Why would his son play video games constantly and his daughter spend so much time on Instagram instead of reading? He had little patience for them and got frustrated when he tried to help them with their homework. He didn't understand play. They had no ambition. They weren't driven the way he was, and he despaired for their future. Because he was typically compulsive, he focused on what they were doing "wrong" and needed fixing—not what they were doing right.

The kids felt all of this. They admired him, but they also feared him. It seemed impossible to please him. Since he didn't say much, they always assumed he was angry—even when he wasn't. He didn't seem to them to have much fun. How could being a lawyer be fun? They were determined not to be like him since he seemed so unhappy.

His son chose to rebel by using drugs. At his age (fourteen) he could see no reason to try to be like his father or follow his rules. He felt no love from him. His daughter (twelve) became bulimic. While bulimia may be partially caused by biological irregularities, circumstances such as those in Ted's home will make the situation far worse. It appeared that Ted didn't care. The truth is that he was so confused by the problems, and so afraid of them, that he used his usual strategy of avoidance, justifying working longer hours, telling himself they needed the money to pay for their treatment. He actually felt they were better off without him around. He found excuses not to attend the family therapy sessions all the doctors had suggested. Underneath it all he felt he was failing as a father, but couldn't face it.

Parenting

As either the direct caretaker or as the financial provider, you've got a great excuse to be compulsive. Note carefully—that's an excuse, not a reason. Whether that means excessive washing and cleaning, or working late at the office, some parents try to justify engaging in compulsive behavior that they find gratifying by rationalizing that their family needs them to do it. This is another example of good energy being hijacked for bad causes. No one in your family wants you to be an unhealthy compulsive. You have the opportunity to model hard work and self-reliance for your children. But you are at risk of demonstrating being a slave to work and a joyless existence.

One opportunity for you if you are raising children is to have a second chance at experiencing play. Most driven people became serious at a fairly early age and didn't have what we might call a typical childhood. Play for you may have been throwing as many fastballs as you could before your shoulder wore out. Or dutifully reading the complete works of Emily Dickinson. Or learning how the stock market works. That's all fine and well, but it left out more free and imaginative play, play that could enrich you if you engage in it with your children.

Your compulsive tendencies can be a blessing or a curse for your children. On the one hand your organizational skills will guarantee that they're provided for, that deadlines are never missed, and that they get to school on time without being covered in strawberry jam. But if you expect your child to be as reasonable, methodical, and meticulous as you are, you're in for a long painful slog that could make them very unhappy, and—not unlikely—rebel against your attempts to teach them how to make it in the world.

Perhaps one of the biggest mistakes that compulsives make with their kids is expecting them to be mature prematurely.[5] Haste makes waste. You were probably arranging the kitchen cabinets for your parents at seven years, and your seven-year-old is doing his utmost to destroy any order you've tried to impose. He might even be trying to bring a little pandemonium into your overly ordered life. Don't compare him to yourself. Not everyone develops the capacity for organization and persistence as quickly as you did. It doesn't mean he won't. It's just more likely that he will do it on a more typical timeline.

This is especially true with teenagers. They may look like adults, but their brains aren't mature and fully online until they're about twenty-six. This doesn't mean you shouldn't expect more of them as they grow older, but it does mean that they need your consistent, matter-of-fact and empathic guidance—without the judgment—to reach those expectations. The tendency is to criticize them as lazy, foolish, or disrespectful, when much of their behavior is better understood as a wiring system that's still under construction. Your compulsiveness can be very helpful here; staying on them to get done what needs to be done. But the tone and attitude with which you do it makes a great deal of difference.

The values you are trying to instill in them are taking root whether it's visible or not. Because it's often not visible, parents tend to pound harder and harder, and the child eventually becomes rigid, too. Or rebels.

Unhealthy compulsives are in danger of using physical punishment with their children. Anger can lead to it, but what makes them more vulnerable to using physical punishment is their sense that it's the right thing to do. But the research is quite clear that spanking and physical abuse actually deter self-control rather than increase it.[6]

Perhaps one of the greatest dangers in compulsives' parenting is that the children feel that love is bestowed conditionally, only when they live up to the standards the parents set. This scenario creates both anxiety (Will I be loved?) and anger (I'm furious that I have to live this way to be loved).

Ted Starts Over

Ted's affair was both painful and infuriating for Dana. After all these years of being patient and tolerant with him, how could he go out and do this? It wasn't like she hadn't been available for sex. He was the one who always had "too much to do." That rejection had been painful enough.

Ted was distraught at the pain he caused Dana, at having gotten out of control, and at having made a mistake. But his work addiction made it difficult to really change. They tried to patch things up. Ted promised he would be more attentive, but it was harder than he expected, and the results just felt like empty gestures to Dana. He wasn't really ready to give up his attachment to work, and the steps he did take weren't enough for Dana to recover. They separated and he got his own apartment.

Once he was out of the house and on his own, Ted started to feel the full weight of what was happening. He'd always taken his family for granted. They had afforded him just enough human presence for him to get by. But once he was really alone, he realized how important they had been to him, and he became very depressed. He also started to become aware of feelings that he'd tried to ignore for years: anger at feeling he had to please others, longing for more freedom and fun, and a longing for a deeper affectionate relationship with someone he respected. He was overwhelmed, and he decided to try therapy.

He had hoped that therapy would help him get his family back, but it was too late for that. Yet his depression was so bad that he was motivated to continue and try to work his way out of it. This meant understanding his story and his strategy, allowing himself to feel things he'd avoided for years, and get clear about what was important to him.

We looked at his past in terms of how it affected his present situation. Having felt a conflict between people and his achievement goals, he'd chosen his achievement goals. He realized that his working late hadn't just been a way to avoid Dana. It was a way to avoid his feelings. While work had been satisfying for him, it had been hijacked by his fears about people and used as a way to avoid them. We questioned his story about the conflict with people: was it really either/or?

With time Ted realized that when he first met Dana he was out of balance, empty in certain areas, and therefore vulnerable to having someone more fun-loving fill the vacuum. He wanted a relationship, and he wanted to be freed from his own severe discipline. He had confused the two—thinking that a relationship with Dana would help him be less compulsive. Out of touch with himself, he hadn't been able to gauge whether he really loved her or he just felt different when he was with her, because he was momentarily freed from his own restrictions. These are very different things. In a way his fling with the young associate was quite similar. A part of him still longed for relationship, but he'd ignored it so completely that it took over the wheel and drove him into the affair. It rebelled against his efforts to be so disciplined.

Ted's psychological work took time and the sort of persistence that he was actually good at. After a period of getting to know himself and recognizing that having a good relationship with someone he really liked and shared his intellectual interests was important to him, he began dating another woman. He learned to say what he wanted and what he didn't want so that he could connect without sacrificing his authenticity, or his goals, for his relationship.

As he became more comfortable with his own feelings, he began to understand his children better. While being the noncustodial parent is never easy, he came to actively value his relationships with them by spending time with them and taking more of a role in their life.

Summary

- Accept that people have different roles to play in the world. Yours might be to speed things up, others to slow things down. In order to have good relationships, you may need to compromise and slow down your tempo when you're with other people.
- Set an intention to notice things you like or enjoy about other people. Don't focus on what you think of as their shortcomings.
- Find as many opportunities as you can to affirm people for what they're doing well.
- Decide if and how much you want people to be a part of your life. Don't socialize out of obligation, but also don't imagine that relationships are an either/or proposition. People who are a good fit for you will understand your need for work—within reason.
- If you do decide to make people more of a priority in your life, schedule more time with them. It may not feel good at first, and you may not always be in the mood. But if you change your behavior first, your feelings will follow. This strategy is more effective once you're aware of what's going on in the background. You might not always feel like socializing, but if you have some insight about how you got off track, and then take the first step to socialize, you'll probably feel better once you get there.
- Learn to set boundaries inside of relationships rather than setting them so high that no one gets in. It's OK to say: "Sure. I'd love to go out to dinner, but I'll need to meet (or leave) at 8:30."
- When you feel that other people are getting in the way of your productivity or perfectionism, and you begin to get impatient or critical, ask yourself, "What's most important to me?"
- Consider whether your caring about other people has actually led you to judge them. Are people still people to you, or have they become obstacles or vehicles to you achieving your goals? Have you confused the means (productivity or righteousness) with the ends?
- Try to get a sense of how you actually come across to other people. Ask the people you are closest to how they see you. Take what they have to say seriously. See if you can find some truth in it. Imagine what it would feel like to be your child, parent, partner,

employee, or friend. You may project an entirely different attitude to people than what you feel inside.

- Ask yourself whether you have wanted your partner to live out your less compulsive side. If the relationship is going to thrive, and if either of you are going to grow psychologically, you'll need to take on some of the qualities that the other, nondriven, person has been living out for you. She or he may need to take over the budgeting, and you may need to start letting a few more feelings slip out. You may find that if you let loose some, they'll start to tighten up a bit more—in a healthy way.

- Identify and appreciate differences you have with your partner. Steer your energy toward the project of making your relationship better.

- Identify buttons that your kids might push in you and set intentions to breathe slowly and deeply rather than to react. What are the issues that are most likely to make you angry? When these come up, you may be the one who needs a time-out rather than your child.

- Identify any ways that you may be setting unrealistic expectations for your children. Deal consciously with any disappointment you may have that they don't seem to be as ambitious or driven as you are. Do you convey to them that your love is conditional or unconditional?

- Remember that as a parent you're always planting seeds in your children. Don't expect these seeds to bear fruit for years or even decades. Be mindful of the types of seeds you are planting: impatient, angry, and judgmental, or reassuring, confident, and supportive?

CHAPTER TWELVE

Rest and Play

I am a compulsive worker. But I'm also a compulsive relaxer.

—A. Scott Berg

Meredith

Meredith, a documentary film producer, struggled with leisure. It's true that documentary films are always a labor of love, and to make a living at it you have to be persistent, but she could never let it go. She began to feel very anxious whenever she wasn't engaged in a productive task. She looked quite strong to people on the outside, but with no work to dive into, she experienced a nameless dread. When she wasn't working on a film, she engaged in local politics, organized the house, jogged, or served on her son's school's PTA.

But she was starting to get worn down by her relentless schedule, as was her family. Her husband kept telling her they all needed a break. She resisted at first but eventually agreed to a vacation in a year, once she had finished the projects she was working on. In typical driven style, Meredith meticulously planned the perfect vacation over the next year, reading every review for every possible location, hotel, and outing. She didn't really trust her husband to get it right, and she actually enjoyed the diversion. But at the same time, she was setting herself up for disappointment by trying to make it perfect.

She had imagined with her two films finished her desk would be clear and she'd be able to relax. It didn't happen that way. It rarely does. A new project came her way two weeks before they left, and trying to get the initial work done before they left ended up making the household so frantic that her husband and son wondered whether it was worth it to go.

Once they got to the hotel, they found that the internet was down, and Meredith wasn't able to even check her email, much less get any work done. So much for the perfect vacation. She complained bitterly to the hotel manager, though the issue wasn't their fault and there was nothing to be done. Never come between a driven person and her projects.

She started to get irritable with her husband, who was content to sit on the beach and enjoy the warm breeze. He wouldn't validate her frustration about the internet being inaccessible: "Meredith, get over it. This may just be one of the best things that's ever happened to you. Or us. Come have a drink with me." She joined him, but she still couldn't relax. She felt an urgent need to make the most of every second—doing and exploring things she couldn't do at home.

She had especially looked forward to taking their twelve-year-old son, Danny, snorkeling. Danny had a fantasy of being a marine biologist, and snorkeling would be heaven for both of them. Meredith had scheduled a tour that was supposed to include fishing and snorkeling. Only after leaving shore did it become apparent that there would be no snorkeling—something about damaged reefs. Meredith was furious and wanted to find some way to get back at the tour guide for ruining her gift to her son.

Opportunities

Here's a scientifically proven fact that every driven person should learn to love: time away from work helps you to be more creative and productive.[1] Rest is just as essential to doing good work as persistence is. Really. Your brain doesn't stop working on a problem if you lie in a hammock for eleven minutes. In fact, you're actually more likely to come up with a solution to that snag you've been blocked by. Once you stop focusing on the problem consciously, an entirely different part of your brain springs into action to work on the problem. Remember the instinctual Self 2 of Timothy Gallwey and Carl Jung that I spoke of in the preface? This is it. It often reaches far better solutions than Self 1 with its drive and determination.[2] So, ironically, neglecting rest means you miss an opportunity to be more productive.

But you've gotta give rest a chance. Part of vacation is letting someone else do the driving for a change. Give your poor tired executive function a rest before it crashes. Even mind-wandering—heaven forbid—can lead to more creative solutions.[3] Rest and distraction allow you to turn off your hyperdeveloped critical function so that the brain's creative function, the constructive unconscious, can work its magic for a little while.[4] Your ideas need time to incubate. Rest presents an opportunity for wisdom and guidance from other parts of your psyche to inform your driving. Don't blame it for not helping if you never give it time to work.

Similarly, play can also improve social skills, increase productivity and creativity, prevent burnout, and decrease depression.

But if you rest and play solely to get better at work, your value system is still askew, and you're missing one of the more enjoyable experiences in life. Psychiatrist and play researcher Stuart Brown lists purposelessness as one of the defining characteristics of play.[5] If you rest just to get ahead, rest becomes a necessary evil without really changing the balance of your psyche. Similarly, if you play simply to sharpen your skills so that when you go out into the real world you're more effective, there is no real change of attitude.

Rest and play are best appreciated as pleasurable ends in themselves. While play originally had a role in our evolution and survival, it now has its own neurochemical reward system: joy.

True play is fun, spontaneous, unselfconscious, pleasurable, and surprising. Different people have different approaches to getting there. Here are eight play personality types that Brown suggests: the Joker, the Kinesthete (who needs to move his or her body), the Explorer, the Competitor, the Director, the Collector, the Artist/Creator, the Storyteller. Identifying your own approach will help you to access it more easily.

Dangers

Neglect

The first danger with rest and play is that you don't take advantage of them. If you're compulsive, you're probably very good at delaying gratification. Because you delay it until the lists are all checked off, and lists never end, you'll probably never get around to allowing yourself "re-creation."

If you don't have healthy ways of relaxing and enjoying yourself, you're vulnerable to getting pulled in to destructive forms of them, substitutes for more sustainable leisure: drugs, alcohol, shopping, and pornography addictions can all take over when you don't have a more conscious way to kick back. The child is going to get what it wants. The question is how skillfully that's going to happen.

Affairs are especially seductive if you don't have a healthier way to enjoy life. Recall the example of Ted, the work-addicted attorney who was drawn first to his wife, and then to an affair with an associate, because they each seemed to offer him some relief from his compulsive work habits. The other person becomes an escape from the grind— someone who shows you kindness and sensitivity and helps you engage in the pleasure that you never learned to offer yourself. Someone who treats you the way you should be treating yourself. The point here is not a moral one but a psychological one: if you don't consciously find a way to unwind, you may do it unconsciously, and the results won't satisfy for long. Consciously examining your motivations may save you grief. Are you interested in the person because you enjoy, respect, and admire him or her, or because he or she does something for you that you haven't learned to do for yourself? You may still decide to have an affair, but first see what you imagine the person will do for you.

Not resting and relaxing can make you angry, self-righteous, and resentful of those who do make time for themselves. Not allowing yourself respite and pleasure makes you vulnerable to soaking in your victimhood, feeling like you're better because you suffer more. This substitute indulgence can become masochistic.

Perfectionism

Another danger in regard to rest and play is that you become as per-fectionistic about them as you are about everything else. Dinner with friends becomes a command performance. Watching a movie becomes a test of intellect. Sex becomes an athletic contest.

Take vacations, for example. They can be just as trying for compulsives as work—in fact probably even more so. Compulsives are set up for failure in this area: they're programmed for productivity and perfection—neither of which cohabit well with vacation. Depending on the type of vacation you take, chances are it's not totally predictable or controllable. If things don't go as planned, driven people tend to have a hard time letting go and enjoying what there is to enjoy.

But perhaps worse, they can become critical of their own struggle to have fun. "I know I should be enjoying myself, and I'm not, so I'm failing—again"—which leads to a downward spiral that's hard to reverse.

Lots of driven people enjoy the challenges and the opportunity for mastery that sports, games, and puzzles offer. At least the healthy ones do. The unhealthy ones take the competition too seriously and all the fun goes out of it. Play loses its charm, innocence, and lightheartedness. It's less fun for the people around them, too.

Invasion of the Killer Devices

Work is mobile now. Clothed in the disguise of sleek, harmless, and sexy machines, it seeps and creeps into all the places that used to be work-free and set aside for respite and re-creation. Compulsives are especially vulnerable to this infection.

The ancient Greeks created and carefully maintained places referred to as Temenoi—sacred spaces set aside for worship, reflection, and healing. Cell phones, watches, computers, tablets, and abacuses were all strictly forbidden. They knew the value of setting aside a time and a place free from common worries and concerns. They knew intuitively that a Temenos allows us to stop the constant flow of the stress hormone cortisol, which, if uninterrupted, literally kills off brain cells.

But Temenos is a rare find now.

Without such time and space guarded from devices and their addictive and deadly qualities, it's difficult to engage in the leisure and relaxation so necessary for our well-being. Every time your body starts to settle down and withdraw from the habit of checking and fixing, there is another click or bing or ring that you feel enslaved to respond to.

Beware the killer devices.

Meredith Learns That Rest Pays Off

Recall that Meredith was on the tour boat with her family and had just gotten the news that there would be no snorkeling that day. Noticing that her anger felt familiar, and remembering how bad she had felt whenever she had expressed it vindictively, she paused and asked herself what was more important: her mood, or punishing the tour guide for getting in the way of her goal? What did she want to model for their son? Righteousness, or handling disappointment gracefully? After a single comment to the operator, Meredith let it go. Better put, she gave up. She realized she just wasn't going to be able to control everything and she might as well try to enjoy what there was to enjoy. Thus ensued the inner battle for Meredith's vacation.

She went through withdrawal for two days. She went cold turkey on control, perfection, and work. At first lying on the beach was torture. Up. Down. Up. Down. She couldn't be still. She got upset with herself for not being able to let go. But eventually, and ironically, letting it all go, relaxing, became her project, her work. Eventually she was able to slow down enough to begin to really feel the difference between the relentless pace at which she was usually driven, and a calmer, slower pace in which she could savor. Ideas about the new film she was working on kept popping up. She learned to make a note and leave it alone.

She gave in and played cards with her husband and son. Her son teased her about goofing off. He teased her about how badly she needed to win. Clearly he was enjoying her more relaxed state. She laughed at herself.

She listened—really listened—to music on her headphones on the beach. She recalled the pleasure music had brought her when she was young, far more pleasure than when it served just as ubiquitous background or motivation to run faster.

On the plane ride home she took out her notes and realized how much "work" she'd gotten done while not working. Issues that had been problematic before vacation now seemed workable. Her ideas quickly coalesced in a way they hadn't when she was focused on it twelve hours a day.

Even a compulsive can learn to relax on vacation. The real challenge for Meredith was to find a way to balance things once she got home. She recalled how helpful the vacation had been for her project and started making a point of taking short breaks each day, and longer breaks on the weekend. She started to trust that she could work without working. But more importantly, she realized how rest and play were enjoyable in themselves—not just means to an end.

Summary

- Don't just do something: sit there. For you, doing nothing is doing something.
- Consume humor. Movies, theater, jokes, and stand-up comedians all help break the death grip the unhealthy compulsive has on the steering wheel.
- Learn to savor peace, relaxation, taste, sound, sensation, and beauty.
- Identify ways of relaxing and finding pleasure that are a good fit for you.
- Make a realistic plan to implement these and stick with it. If it helps to get started moving in this direction, put "relax" on your list and check it off each time you do it. But ideally, eventually these things will be enjoyable in themselves, rather than something you can check off your list.
- Notice the feelings that come up when you stop working. You'll probably be nervous at first. That's OK. Make a mental note of the fear. Exhale. Soothe the frightened child and return to rest.
- Alternate time at your desk with time walking, stretching, or speaking with friends.
- When you do set aside time to relax, play, or take vacation, leave the perfectionism behind. Accept yourself and your situation as you are, including your difficulty in relaxing. Set an intention at the outset to make being present to whatever happens the priority, rather than having it be perfect. It needs to be more important to you to be sane than to get things just right.

CHAPTER THIRTEEN

Psychological Growth

Vicissitudes of the Inner Game

We must forgo compulsion and turn to self-development.

—Carl Jung

Cindy

Cindy was on the verge of a professional tennis career at the age of twenty-two when she had a serious injury to her shoulder. She underwent surgery and worked hard at rehab, but eventually she had to acknowledge that she would not be able to keep playing at a professional level.

She'd started playing at six years old. When most of the other kids were tired and goofing off on the courts, she'd still be energetic and determined to improve her game. As she grew older, she practiced compulsively, often without resting enough, which was one reason that she injured her shoulder and that it didn't heal well enough to continue playing. She was ambitious. She was always trying to advance her game, and sometimes it set her back. This was also true psychologically. If she missed a shot, she'd get down on herself and then miss more shots. It was a different sort of injury, but at least as destructive.

She was the third of four children. Her oldest brother was an academic star at school but disengaged from the family. Her older sister

141

was dramatically gorgeous but fought constantly with her parents for freedom. Her younger brother had leukemia and was constantly in and out of the hospital. Her working-class parents were already stressed by finances and were even more stressed by her brother's illness. Cindy felt a need to find something to be recognized for and to bring something positive to her parents' lives. She enjoyed tennis, and she loved the challenge of getting better at it. She also used tennis to feel good about herself, and to feel that she had something to offer. It helped her to feel less dwarfed by her siblings, and to feel that she was giving her parents something to feel good about. Because the stakes were so high, she became very hard on herself. She developed a severe inner critic that accused her of slacking off, of not being committed, of not focusing, and of not having any talent.

Her family didn't have the means to send her to one of the special tennis academies that the wealthier kids went to, so she attended public school and practiced after classes. This required that she maintain a one-track mind. Much of her time was spent traveling to the courts where she practiced. Friends and boyfriends didn't fit into her schedule. School would have interested her, but she was focused on her game.

She won a scholarship to college and began working her way up the national rankings ladder. But in her senior year she injured her shoulder. This happened shortly after her brother died of leukemia. She finished her degree and moved back home to figure out her next step.

Cindy was devastated, and for the first time in her life she began to fall into a depression. She'd spent her life living in the future, preparing for a tennis career, and now that that was over she had no idea what to do. She worked at a sporting goods store, selling racquets to other people. She got herself to her job, but was listless, restless, and moody. The energy that had gone into tennis couldn't find an outlet. With no other choices, she had to focus that energy on her emotional well-being in order to rebuild her life. It was move forward or backward. She chose to move forward.

The Instinct toward Psychological Growth and Its Trivialization

Our final fulcrum issue is far less tangible and therefore often goes unseen and unconscious; the energy it carries often goes undirected and awry. It's experienced more in your inner life than in your outer world, but it's no less important. It is the internal motivation for personal psychological growth, the balanced expansion of the personality, and it provides the very energy that fuels your driven personality—for better or worse. The drive you feel to achieve externally is a manifestation of a deeper instinct.

The humanistic psychologists called it the drive to self-actualization.[1] Carl Jung called it individuation.[2] Timothy Gallwey called it the Inner Game. When we master challenges[3] and achieve competence[4] we find it satisfying because they fulfill the urge toward personal growth. Warriors, saints, heroes, and heroines of all kinds have symbolized this instinct to character development that exists in all cultures and in all periods. It is the archetype of all archetypes.

I began this book sharing my experience learning about how both Gallwey and Jung spoke about Self 1 and Self 2, Self 2 being the natural, instinctual part of us that ideally provides the directions for our driving. This Self 2 is the source of this urge toward growth.

Because Nature loves diversity, psychological growth leads to different goals for different people at different stages in their lives. It could include developing the ability to bond or to be independent, to fight and speak one's piece or to be flexible and accept limitations, to create the new or to savor what is, to experience a wider range of emotions or to rein them in when necessary, to experience pride or to embrace humility, to be realistic or to dream what had been unthinkable. The underlying theme is an expansion of the personality that fosters adaptation to a wider set of circumstances. When we are engaged in this process, we feel encouragement, fulfillment, and momentum.

While growth may occur and be expressed through interactions with the outer world, the deeper motivation is the development of character, inner work in which we make changes to ourselves as we make changes to the outer world. Whatever manifestations this drive may take, the ongoing development of the human personality through the integration of as many psychological potentials as possible may be one of the oldest and most deeply embedded urges in our evolutionary psychic heritage.

Some evolutionary biologists argue that evolution is not random. Rather it is progressive and directional, moving toward complexity, cooperation, and adaptivity. Cells divide and specialize. Diversify or die. These cells then work together in order to adapt and survive in a greater diversity of settings and situations. Similarly, psychological complexity increases when we develop different parts of ourselves that specialize in certain tasks. Those parts then work together in greater cooperation to make us more flexible and robust. This tendency toward development occurs throughout the spectrum of life, from the level of single cells to that of far more complex organisms and communities.[5]

This ancient tendency remains a part of who we are and is experienced in our personal tendency toward psychological development. Driven people seem to carry more than a typical share of it, and therefore are at risk of becoming its victim if it's not integrated consciously.

But the call to "become our best selves" has become ubiquitous, and its popularity, I fear, has trivialized something that is actually quite vital and profound. It might seem trite, optional, or cosmetic. But whether you respect it or not, the pull to psychological growth is there.

As with all the other fulcrum issues, the urge to grow psychologically can lead to fulfillment or misery, depending on how consciously we steer it. Personal growth partially fills the need for meaning we explored as the third step in a plan to become a healthier compulsive. But if this urge drives us mindlessly, it takes us to a dead end.

Opportunities

If we can become conscious of the Inner Game, it helps us to undertake all the external challenges we're faced with while putting them in perspective. There is less pressure for external achievement, but no less desire. We are less attached to outcome and more engaged in process. Achievement no longer feels like a matter of life or death. In fact, with this perspective we can use the occasions when we don't "succeed" as opportunities for growth.[6]

Turning your endlessly creative energy toward the development of your personality can also balance your urge to make your mark in the outer world. It may help you to have more of a sense of control by focusing on your inner world when the outer world won't bend to your will. In some ways, though not all, your personality is more malleable than the world. This is not to say that turning our attention inward is a retreat. It can actually be more difficult.

Inner and outer projects need not be exclusive. In fact, I'd say that we are at our best when they are in balance.

If consciously cultivated, this urge for psychological growth becomes a source of meaning that gives a clear, healthy, and manageable direction to your life. Many patients have told me that what helps sustain and motivate them through challenges is their sense of momentum, knowing that they are engaged in the development of their personality. When they need to let go of judgment, anger, resentment, overworking, or overcontrolling, they can hold to a motivation that is especially strong for the driven person—the realization of personal potential.

The rich literature of heroes and heroines shows them overcoming not just external challenges, but also challenges within themselves. In fact, it's often overcoming the inner challenges that allows them to overcome the outer challenges. After a bout of destructive rage Hercules was forced to take on the infamous Ten Labors. In order to accomplish these labors, he had to discipline his own unruly personality. These labors required him to submit to someone else, which required him to develop self-control. Slaying monsters was easy for him compared to working on his own personality.

This powerful sense of becoming may well be what accounts for the fact that most forms of psychotherapy are effective, at least to some extent. All forms of therapy both encourage and tap into this potential.

Psychologist and researcher Carol Dweck of Stanford University has put a fine point to this fulcrum issue and called it "growth mindset." Dweck's extensive research validates the benefits of an outlook in which we see ourselves as capable of growth, rather than having a fixed and limited capacity.[7] Those who believe that intelligence and character are qualities that can be changed and developed fare far better than those who see themselves as having set potential. It seems to be the mind-set that most accounts for change rather than the talents they may be born with.

Valuing this inner project may also be the only satisfying solution to aging and the inevitable infirmity and limitations that come with it.

Dangers

But our drive for growth also has its dangers. It's a particularly decisive issue for people who are driven. Because they seem to have an especially strong urge for growth, it can become either very beneficial or very damaging. There is a shadow side to this urge; if it isn't engaged consciously and in a balanced way, it can take over the wheel and drive us crazy.

Displacement

The first danger for people who are driven is that they sometimes displace the urge for inner work onto an external goal and miss the possibilities inherent in the Inner Game. In themselves, external projects aren't bad; the question is whether they exclude or blind us to the important possibilities of personal growth. Here are some examples of what this looks like:

You build a small empire of grocery stores. You make money and people get the food they need. But if you don't also feed your soul, the business distracts from an aspect of your inner life that needs your attention. Your emotional and relational life shrink and you become a cranky old man or woman.

You break sales records at your company for ten years by showing people the value of your company's product. But if you don't value your own self, you miss the inner urge. Things may look good on the outside, but inside you feel empty. You become depressed.

You win a bicycle race and get a prize and lots of attention. But if you fail to put energy into your own balance and momentum, you may miss the point of your journey. You move so fast you never savor the moment or find meaning in what you're doing.

External achievements can be satisfying and benefit the greater good, but if they exclude working on psychological issues, the victories may not satisfy for long. If you didn't have a good fit with your environment when you were young, your drive for psychological growth may have been hijacked and diverted to outer projects to placate caretakers or society, and to prove to yourself and others that you're good enough. The energy meant for inner work is siphoned off.

Unhealthy compulsives are known for trying to avoid emotions by focusing on practical problems. So, for instance, if the challenges of inner growth are daunting, you may displace the problem onto your outer world. If your inner challenge is to learn to clear out old resentments, you may avoid it by starting a litter cleanup campaign in your town. This doesn't have to be an either/or, proposition. Ideally it's a both/and. The outer projects will go better once the inner problem has begun to be addressed because you stop obsessing desperately about it. Goals then emerge out of desire and intrinsic motivation rather than anxiety and extrinsic motivation. You're also less likely to burn out your engine by spinning your wheels if you're paying attention to what's going on inside of you. You're more likely to be a healthy compulsive if you also have awareness of the inner project.

Religion can, and often does, serve as a healthy support for the development of character. But some forms of religion, with their emphasis on self-purification and life in the hereafter, offer the compulsive a ready-made substitute for the urge toward individuation. A prescribed path toward "goodness" that requires hard work, self-sacrifice, and adherence to dogma and rules may seem to many driven people like an ideal way out of difficult decisions.

Living in the Future

Another danger is that when the drive for growth gets hijacked by insecurity, self-improvement feels so imperative that you don't live in the present. If you use personal growth to prove that you're worthy, then the personality may be so completely controlled by "becoming" that you have no sense of "being," no sense of living in the present or savoring it. Workshops, self-help books, trainings, diets, and austere practices may promise that with enough hard work you'll eventually become that person you've always wanted to be. Constantly leaning forward into the future, you think and do everything with the hope that someday you'll reach a higher level of being. This is quicksand for the compulsive.

Perfectionism and Self-criticism

This deep urge to grow, hijacked by insecurity and driven by perfectionism, can lead to intense self-criticism, depression, burnout, or procrastination.[8] You may feel that you aren't making enough progress toward your ideals, and fall into the habit of using shame to try to coerce better results. This usually backfires. Acceptance of yourself as you are is much more effective in moving forward than shaming. Once basic self-acceptance is in place, then we can acknowledge how we can do better. But not before. Compulsives tend to put the cart before the horse: "I'll accept myself once I get better," which is a recipe for a downward spiral.

Self-Preoccupation

The search for personal growth can also lead to self-preoccupation: it leads some to become so intent on their psychological development that they forget that their actions have an impact on other people. When this happens, individualism replaces individuation and leaves out not only other parts of the personality, but also other human beings.

As *New York Times* editorial columnist David Brooks wrote,

> Instead of seeing the self as the seat of the soul, the meritocracy sees the self as a vessel of human capital, a series of talents to be cultivated and accomplishments to be celebrated. If you base a society on a conception of self that is about achievement, not character, you will wind up with a society that is demoralized; that puts little emphasis on the sorts of moral systems that create harmony within people, harmony between people and harmony between people and their ultimate purpose.[9]

When the drive for growth gets hijacked by fear, it may exclude the natural motivation to bond with and care for others. There is room within the drive for psychological growth for generosity, community, and altruism. These qualities best emerge organically from a balanced, secure, psyche rather than from being conscripted into action to defend fragile self-esteem.

Cindy Finds a Place for Her Drive

When Cindy began therapy, one of our first tasks was to question the internal voice that constantly criticized her, and to question specifically the idea that she had failed. The critical voice targeted all her actions from small to large, but most of all she blamed herself for causing her injury by practicing without rest. I told her that her new job was to accept herself and what she had done first, before she could begin to think about what she might do differently going forward. When I put it that way I could see her gears starting to turn: "Oh, a new goal." The idea of not blaming herself wasn't new, but that she could redirect her energy into her emotional rehabilitation, and even more optimistically, her psychological growth, seemed to turn on a small light of hope. In fact, without attention to her psychological growth she would probably have remained blocked and become more depressed. She needed to learn to break the cycle of self-criticism so that it didn't infect her approach to psychological growth.

Cindy had already developed discipline and resilience; the tragedies of her brother's death and her own injury had forced her to grow up fast. While the prospect of redirecting the energy that had gone into tennis into a psychological goal wasn't exciting in the same way as winning a tournament was, it was highly motivating to her, and offered the possibility of a deeper, more fulfilling satisfaction. She had a sense of direction again, but this time it was different; it was less frantic and more assured. This time her desire was steering, rather than her fear and self-judgment.

Cindy's challenge in her recovery and growth was to redirect the energy that had gone into tennis toward personal change, and to remain balanced while doing it. This meant she had to integrate aspects of her personality that she had excluded, such as emotions, pleasure, rest, attention to her health, and her need for relationships. She was very determined, and her default habit was to focus intently and exclusively on her progress. To make these changes, Cindy needed to understand her story and how she came to adopt her strategy of self-criticism.

While Cindy had genuinely hoped that her tennis career would be helpful to her parents, she had to acknowledge that her need to succeed had also been motivated by her desire to feel that she was at least as special as her siblings. It was understandable given her situation, but it had left her preoccupied with efforts to become a great tennis player. She had believed that if she focused and pushed herself hard enough, she would succeed and solve her problems and those of her family. That strategy hadn't worked. In fact, she had become isolated and prickly. Going forward, personal growth would need to include self-compassion and forgiveness along with responsibility. She needed to learn to accept that she was going to "miss shots" off the court also. Being present to who she was in the present was just as important as was her drive to move forward.

She also needed to allow herself to feel emotions that she'd been avoiding for years. She looked back with both fondness and sadness at her years of playing. It had been exciting, and when she won a match or a tournament it was very gratifying. But she was also sad at what she had sacrificed while she was playing: friendships, time with her family, and fun. She'd lost her childhood, and it needed to be mourned. She also had to allow herself to feel sad about her brother's passing and her parents' struggle, feelings she had tried to avoid with her determination to succeed. In this area, personal growth meant allowing herself to feel more and more, rather than push feelings away with work.

Another aspect of her growth was to allow herself the time and vulnerability to cultivate relationships. Having lost a brother and a career, Cindy feared that anything else she invested herself in would also eventually disappoint her. But because she could now put this challenge in a larger context of personal growth, she could take more risks, and began to enjoy relationships.

Cindy eventually pursued graduate studies at a state college near her home town. She became a high school guidance counselor, where she was able to use everything she had learned to help the students there. When she had setbacks, she could take them in stride, aware of a larger goal and sense of momentum.

While on the surface this appeared to be a new direction for Cindy, it was really just a growing awareness of a deeper drive that she had experienced unconsciously, but intensely, from a young age. The drive that had only been able to find expression in tennis was now free to flow elsewhere. Now she was able to channel it more consciously, balancing the various parts of her personality, living with less desperation and more desire.

Summary

- Ask yourself whether natural urges for psychological development have:

- been displaced onto external situations.
- kept you from living in the present.
- limited your identity.
- led to perfectionism.
- led to self-preoccupation.
- Develop an intention to consciously value the balanced expansion of your personality.
- Outline what an expansion of your own personality will include.
- Try to become aware of the feeling of satisfaction that growth brings, and savor it each time it occurs.

PART IV

SUPPORT FOR
THE ROAD AHEAD

CHAPTER FOURTEEN

~

Support for the
Compulsive's Journey

Now that you have a better understanding of yourself and you've taken over the wheel, you may still have questions about how to continue moving forward. Compulsive patterns can be very deeply ingrained, and staying on track to becoming a healthier compulsive will benefit from gentle persistence and support. Here are some ways to get the support.

Individual Psychotherapy

The path that I've outlined in this book may be taken with or without a guide, but with support your chances of success are better. While we do have research that says that psychotherapy is effective in achieving a healthier compulsive style, we don't have research that measures the efficacy of a self-directed program of change.

A therapist can be helpful in creating a sense of comfort and security that then allows the two of you to work together to break the habits of thinking, feeling, and behavior typical of the unhealthy compulsive personality. It seems that we're wired to achieve change through relationships. Many of us need another human being to interrupt the patterns and habits that are part of our strategy, which is what the therapeutic relationship does best.

It's not that the therapist tells you exactly what to do and somehow changes your behavior. Rather, the therapeutic situation provides an opportunity to have interpersonal experiences that help us to understand the conditions that led us to develop our strategies for dealing with the world. It also provides opportunities for therapeutic experiences that change how we feel about ourselves, which in turn helps us to change our strategy. Many people are aware of their unhealthy tendencies, but simply trying to will themselves to act more reasonably doesn't always work. This is why the experience of the therapeutic relationship can be so helpful.

For instance, unhealthy compulsives often have difficulty delegating, trusting someone else to do things that are up to their standards. Trusting a therapist for help is a form of delegating. This presents an opportunity to talk about, and work on, some of your challenges (policing, being critical or controlling) in real life—not just theoretically. Yes—you can and should tell your therapist when you think they're wrong, but it also helps to talk about what's pushing your buttons and explore how you respond when your buttons are pushed.

Therapy can also be challenging for the compulsive because it's time consuming. Sitting in session, working on your psychology, actively challenges your ideas about what work is most valuable and most effective. You have to face the feelings you usually avoid when you can't turn to a computer. Instead you process it as it's happening with someone who is trained to help you see and live differently. In the long run, putting aside time for your well-being is a good way to break your addiction to efficiency because you discover that you can tolerate the feeling you've been avoiding. Ironically, it may actually help you to use your time better.

The compulsive tendency is to resort to our default strategies (such as preparing and perfecting) whenever things get difficult. Meeting with a therapist regularly prepares you to recognize these situations as they come up, and makes it more likely that at some point you'll end up in their office just as it's happening so that your therapist can help you identify the tendency to resort to old strategies, and help you to substitute new behaviors.

Therapists also have the advantage of observing you from the outside; they can point out the strategies you use when you feel anxiety, strategies that you may not be able to see from your subjective vantage point. We all rationalize some behavior, and having someone professional notice these behaviors with you can be very valuable. At the same time, therapists model an accepting attitude that can be a much-needed balance to your perfectionism. It's not that they let you off the hook, but they will demonstrate a much less puncturing approach to taking responsibility.

But their role is not just to point out where you are not adapting well. It's also to help you figure out what's most fulfilling for you, and to help you pursue it consciously.[1] Therapy is intended to foster your relationship with your deepest longings, to understand where compulsions originally spring from, and, especially in the case of the driven person, to find a way to honor those longings in a healthy way.

Which Type of Psychotherapy Is Best for Me?

To simplify greatly, there are two broad categories of psychotherapy: cognitive and behavioral therapies (such as CBT), and dynamic and expressive therapies (such as psychodynamic and psychoanalytic). The goals of the two are different. Cognitive and behavioral therapies aim to reduce specific symptoms such as panic attacks, phobias, and depression. Dynamic and expressive therapies aim to make broader changes to the personality.

Here is how psychology researcher Jonathan Shedler, from the University of Colorado School of Medicine, describes the goals of psychodynamic therapy:

> The goals of psychodynamic therapy include, but extend beyond, symptom remission. Successful treatment should not only relieve symptoms (i.e., get rid of something) but also foster the positive presence of psychological capacities and resources. Depending on the person and the circumstances, these might include the capacity to have more fulfilling relationships, make more effective use of one's talents and abilities, maintain a realistically based sense of self-esteem, tolerate a wider range of affect, have more satisfying sexual experiences, understand self and others in more nuanced and sophisticated ways, and face life's challenges with greater freedom and flexibility. Such ends are pursued through a process of self-reflection, self-exploration, and self-discovery that takes place in the context of a safe and deeply authentic relationship between therapist and patient.[2]

So, once again simplifying, if you just want to stop washing your hands compulsively, CBT would probably be effective. But if you want to change your compulsive approach to life, to stop trying to wash your entire life free of imperfections, you may want to consider psychodynamic or expressive therapy.

The approach I've outlined in this book enlists the theories of human change of both approaches, but emphasizes the dynamic view more. Since OCPD affects the entire personality rather than just causing specific symptoms, I believe that the broader ranging approach of dynamic therapy is more helpful.

There is substantial research that validates the effectiveness of dynamic therapies.[3] Dynamic therapies explore how our histories affect us, and whether we are living as if we are still in the past. We use the therapeutic relationship to make these unconscious background motivations more visible and tangible—not just abstract—so that we can have an experience that brings us back into the present. The process of expression that's part of this investigation is also helpful in altering the old narratives that keep us stuck in the past.

Couples' Therapy

Couples' therapy focuses on how you get along with your partner and improving your relationship. Depending on how frequently you meet with your couples' therapist, and how long you attend sessions, you may not have the opportunity to explore much of your history and your personal goals. But it does have other benefits. In couples' therapy your therapist has the advantage of seeing how you actually interact with your partner, and the advantage of getting feedback from your partner about how you relate to him or her, providing information about you that the therapist may not be able to see through just your self-report and his or her own observation in session.

Group Therapy

There are many benefits to participating in groups specializing in compulsive or workaholic patterns: speaking with others who experience the same struggles as you, witnessing your own patterns by seeing them mirrored in others, and getting feedback from others can all be very effective in helping you to break old patterns. Groups can both normalize what you're going through and inspire you to take action in changing your situation. As mentioned in the section above about psychotherapy, people can serve as powerful catalysts in personal change.

While groups that focus specifically on compulsivity can be helpful, other, less specific therapy groups can also help you to pursue the goals that you arrive at in reading this book, such as treating people better, being less controlling, or expressing anger more effectively. Getting feedback from others and making community a larger part of your life can also be healing even if compulsivity is not the central theme of the group.

Affording and Getting to Therapy

But there are real practical issues that make going to psychotherapy difficult. If you don't have enough money to pay for a therapist, or insurance that will help you pay for one, consider attending a clinic or low-fee service provided by a therapeutic training institute. Also, most therapists who work privately are willing to see at least some patients for a reduced fee. It's fine to ask if they do. If you live in a remote area and have difficulty finding a therapist near you, you may want to consider meeting with a therapist via videoconferencing.

Try to find an arrangement that is practical and realistic for you. But beware that compulsive tendencies such as perfectionism and frugality in regard to time and money may cloud your thinking about what you can actually afford.

Support Groups

Other options for support that do not cost money include various forms of support groups.

The twelve-step group Workaholics Anonymous provides support in helping people who are addicted to work to find a better balance in their lives. Participants attend live meetings where they share their struggles and solutions. More experienced participants "sponsor" newer participants by being available to speak, and helping them to work through their twelve steps for recovery.

While not as powerful as being live and in person with others, online forums and support groups for those with OCPD and their loved ones host message boards with resources and discussion that can be helpful. You can read how others have dealt with their issues, post questions, and engage in discussion. Realizing that you are not alone helps to put your struggles into perspective. It can give you the motivation and inspiration to carry out the goals you've set to become healthier.

Meditation

Along with many others, I've found meditation to be very helpful in taking back the wheel of my car, and in understanding where my drive needs to go. But let's talk about what I mean by meditation. I'm not referring to simply sitting still and reflecting. Nor am I referring to just trying to make my mind a blank. I'm referring to a specific method which has been practiced for over two thousand years. Two of the main tools of formal meditation that can be helpful in developing the latent potential of the driven personality are concentration and mindfulness.

When we practice concentration in meditation, we ground our attention on a particular object or process. Most commonly it is the breath, but it can also be the weight of the entire body touching the floor or chair, or counting to ten and backward to zero. Mindfulness, on the other hand, is the awareness of whatever arises in the present moment: thoughts, feelings, and sounds, for instance. As they arise we label thoughts (thinking, remembering, planning, planning, planning . . .), feelings (pleasant or unpleasant, bliss, craving ice cream, hating hunger), or sounds (bird, car, dishes crashing in the kitchen), and then we return to the object of our concentration such as the breath. One of the benefits of mindfulness is an increasing ability to be aware of whatever we feel, without trying to make the feelings go away.

For those of us who are compulsive, this practice can be particularly helpful since it helps us to slow down and be in the present before launching mindlessly into a task. This training of the mind is priceless in everyday functioning; it naturally diminishes angry reactions to the inevitable events that we can't control—without repressing those feelings. But it also helps us to develop the capacity to have a deeper experience of the present, of being able to savor what is right in front of us so that we aren't always leaning desperately into the future, a capacity painfully lacking in the unhealthy compulsive.

Meditation is a way to practice acceptance and letting go, moment to moment. It supports the development of skills that we can call on in challenging moments, including the capacity to release our urge to perfect or control whatever is happening around us.

My own experience has been that Insight or Vipassana Meditation,[4] and a form of Zen meditation developed by Vietnamese monk and activist Thich Nhat Hanh,[5] have been most helpful. But if the religious origins of these forms of meditation are a turnoff for you, consider Mindfulness Based Stress Reduction (MBSR),[6] a secular and research-based form of meditation known to have medical and mental health benefits. You'll need to find an approach that feels like a good fit for you—one that does not amplify your compulsive tendencies or cut you off from your feelings, but rather one that facilitates an awareness of what's going on inside.

Participation in a meditation community can also be helpful. The people with whom we surround ourselves have an impact on us, and if you surround yourself with others who are working toward a more mindful life, it will help you to be more mindful also.

Driving Solo

While we may not have scientific research that says that compulsives can change on their own, certainly people have made changes in their lives for hundreds of years before we invented modern therapy or clinical support groups. But if you decide that you're going to go it alone, there are some issues that you will want to be keenly aware of.

To make such changes on your own will take great concentration, focus, and discipline—all of which you have. However, you've probably used these skills in a much different way than you will need to in order to make changes. It will take far less speed and power, and much more openminded, patient attention to the details of how you think, feel, and behave.

Use your organizing capabilities in the service of change. Be disciplined about being undisciplined. Go ahead and make lists—but the lists will probably have very different content, including health, play, pleasure, leisure, and people. Use the summary lists at the end of each chapter in this book. If it helps, make a check mark each time you engage in new behavior. Use writing in ways that are not so directed. Journaling in a freer form can help you to access the feelings that you will need to understand where you really want to go.

Eventually the motivation for the new behavior will become intrinsic rather than extrinsic: you will enjoy it more for its own sake than for the pleasure of making a check mark. To some extent your feelings will change after you engage in the new behavior.

Most of all it will require that you be honest with yourself about your behavior without being critical. With no one to get feedback from, you will need to develop a part of yourself that can observe your behavior and take responsibility for your actions, but with understanding, compassion, and patience.

CHAPTER FIFTEEN

~

Support and Suggestions for the Compulsive's Partner

If you're compulsive and have a partner, enlisting his or her support in your progress will be essential. Following are some ideas about how he or she can understand and support you in your process. Don't expect him or her to indulge you or pander to your tendencies, but if he or she is pursuing the relationship mindfully, the two of you can work together to make the relationship work.

If you're not compulsive yourself, but are reading this book to understand and help your partner, you're not alone. I probably get just as many requests for help from the partners of people with OCPD as I do from people with OCPD themselves. So, following is an example of someone finding a way to both adapt to her partner and to confront him, to live and communicate with him while still maintaining appropriate boundaries and self-care. Along with the example I'll give more generalized suggestions for partners of compulsives.

Lilly Meets Leonard

Lilly met Leonard while on a vacation. She was a soft-spoken nurse with a surprisingly bawdy sense of humor, an easygoing personality, and a desire for a committed relationship. He was an ambitious salesman with a commanding presence, a lion tattoo on his arm, and a surprisingly soft spot for the underdog. When she first saw him, all she could think about was how perfect he looked. His perfection was later to come back to haunt her. But meanwhile, they launched into a whirlwind, semi-long-distance love affair.

He would do anything for her, it seemed at first. He seemed like such a good guy. He always wanted to do the right thing. He seemed to meet all of her expectations in a relationship: good looks, financial stability, and strong principles. She knew he would never cheat on her. They both lived for the weekends they could get together.

She eventually relocated from Pennsylvania to his town in New Jersey and moved into his apartment with him. But after a few months living together she started to feel uncomfortable. It was becoming clear that not only did he want to do the right thing, he also expected everyone else to. His strong feelings about right and wrong knew no limits: how to clean the house, how to structure sentences, and how Lilly should spend her time. She was often so surprised by his bossiness that she didn't know what to say. While he clearly loved her, he could also be rude and critical. He worked constantly. She told her friends that he seemed to be less interested in spending time between the sheets with her and more and more time alone with his spreadsheets. She wondered if she should move back home.

Three Ways to Improve Your Relationship to a Compulsive

People at the unhealthy end of the compulsive spectrum can be demanding, cold, punishing, angry, and critical. They often cause great distress for their partners, families, friends, and coworkers. If you're in this situation, you may feel like you're getting run over, rejected, or abandoned. It's very hard to live or work with someone who isn't aware of their condition and who's convinced they're right all the time. Even those who are closer to the healthy end of the spectrum can be challenging because of their focus on perfection and production at the expense of relationship.

But with understanding, support, and their own work on their issues, compulsives can also make great partners: reliable, loyal, consistent, hardworking, and committed. Getting to this point, however, can be very difficult, depending on the severity of their symptoms. Because you can't coerce them into change, it often seems impossible to make any progress in improving the relationship.

Nevertheless, there is still much that you can do from your end to improve your situation and the relationship. This is in no way meant to blame you for the issues in the relationship, but rather to point out what is within your control to change, and help you focus on that. If you want to save your relationship, you may need to take a leading and heroic role in breaking negative cycles. What I suggest may seem entirely unfair to you, and it may well be. But given that compulsives are usually not very skilled at relationships, you may need to take the lead in improving yours.

In the most extreme cases of OCPD there may be little that you can do other than encourage him or her to go to couples' or individual therapy, and to set boundaries so that you don't make the situation worse or get hurt. You may not be able to turn it around on your own. Therapy is more likely to be effective in these cases than going it on your own because compulsives can be so adamant about being right. You may need a mental health professional to intervene. Some compulsives feel more comfortable beginning with couples' therapy, while others feel more comfortable beginning with individual therapy. Either mode may help him or her to eventually enter the other mode. But since it can be hard to get someone with OCPD to go to either type of therapy, I'll talk about how to encourage him or her to do so later in this chapter.

Here are the three main changes that you can make to improve your situation:

- Change how you perceive your partner.
- Change how you communicate with your partner.
- Change how you live your own life and take care of yourself.

None of these three changes is enough in itself to turn things around, but the three can work together in a powerful way. We'll go through these individually and follow Lilly as an example of how to apply these suggestions to an actual relationship.

Perception

Appreciate the Good, and Get Out of Right and Wrong

Perspective is a big part of any relationship. To some degree you can choose what characteristics of your partner to focus on. If you can remember the good things they bring to the table, it will help both of you immensely. What attracted you to them in the first place? What strengths do they already bring to the relationship? Balancing the checkbook? Paying bills on time? Providing financially? Upkeep of your home? Cleanliness? Order? Making sure that your family is compliant with the rules that come with renting an apartment, owning a home or car, traveling, or sending a child to school?

If you see your partner as the problem, look again. Stuck relationships are more often the result of collisions between different personalities than one partner being all right and the other all wrong. Look at it this way: compulsives feel that control and efficiency—not gentleness or understanding—are the best ways to get things done, and they can be quite successful at achieving some pretty honorable goals because of their approach. You might approach life entirely differently, and it might seem that your values are entirely different, but it may be more because you try to reach those goals in very different ways. If you want to try to work out the relationship, you may need to see what underlying goals you share, and consider that perhaps the totally different way the compulsive in your life approaches those goals isn't all bad. If each of you feels that your own way is the right way, that's part of the problem.

While compulsives can be cold and rigid, what they seek isn't all wrong. Think of it this way: they're trying to do what they think is the right thing, but they're far too adamant and inflexible in how they achieve it. They feel an extraordinary sense of duty to try to enforce what they see as the right thing to do. They feel there's only one way to do it. As sanctimonious and righteous as they are about their principles, their behavior comes from their sense of obligation to enforce rules that are meant to help.

If you can consider that both of your approaches have their merits, you have a better chance of improving the relationship. Instead of thinking that one of you must be the problem, think in terms of differences. Put the problem outside of the two of you, and turn your attention on "it," the conflict caused by your differing approaches and needs. Neither you nor your partner is the problem; the challenge presented by your fit is the issue.

Look Beneath the Surface to Feelings

Another helpful way to reframe your perspective is to try to look beneath behavior to his or her feelings. This will help you separate the person from the defenses. Unrealistic demands and criticism are the way he or she tries to cope with a disturbing inner world, not his or her essence. Think of that as an external layer of protection, a suit of armor covering someone who wants to do the right thing but is taken over by anxiety and insecurity. Underneath the blustery exterior is probably the fear that he or she won't meet expectations, his own or those of others. He or she may also be experiencing shame—the sense of being deeply and fundamentally flawed, not just that he or she has something wrong, but that he or she is defective. It may be hard to imagine how anxiety provoking this is.

Even when he or she seems to have it all together, underneath he or she probably feels very vulnerable. Keeping in mind what's underneath the surface will help you not take it personally and to find better solutions.

His or her need to have things a certain way intensifies if he or she sees your cooperation—or lack thereof—as an indication of how much you care. Many unhealthy compulsives did not achieve a secure sense of attachment in their families, and they're often hyperalert to the possibility of being abandoned. If you aren't as meticulous as they are, they may feel that it means that you don't care about them. Most compulsives won't say: "Would you please load the dishwasher the way I think it should be because it helps me to deal with my anxiety, and it reassures me that you love me?" But this is often exactly what's going on. If you can look beneath their behavior to their underlying feelings, you may be able to address their needs without giving in to unrealistic demands.

Lilly Changes Her Perspective

As Lilly wondered about leaving Leonard, she recalled her history of leaving relationships quickly when she felt that her expectations weren't met—without trying to work it out. She knew on some level that she either slipped into total dependence and compliance or ran like the wind the other way. There was no middle ground for her, no sense of what it meant to rely on someone in a healthy, interdependent way. She'd bend and bend and bend without complaint until she abruptly broke off the relationship. It really was hurtful to be disappointed yet again, but she suspected that things weren't always the way she interpreted them. Neither of these guys had been saints, but she had wondered if in some cases she could have handled things differently.

When she slowed down, she realized how important it was to Leonard to up his game at work so that he could buy a house for them. She also knew that Leonard was actually insecure underneath his demeanor and was afraid he wouldn't live up to company projections. While Leonard was rude at times, it really didn't mean what it felt like it meant to her—that he didn't really love her. She had to refocus her attention on what he did do right, and what was really going on inside of both of them. She learned that sometimes when he became controlling she could find a way to address the emotional issue beneath the surface: she tried to find ways to reassure him that she cared about him and that he was doing well at his job. Sometimes it worked. She saw their differences and appreciated them, trying not to get caught up in blaming him. They each had a lot to offer the relationship. This helped her to calm down, but it wasn't going to be enough to turn things around. Changing her perspective was necessary but not sufficient.

Communication

Compulsives aren't known for their communication skills. They don't realize how they come across, and, because they're often preoccupied with getting things done, they aren't always aware of the impact they have on others. They constantly charge forward, leaving their loved ones in the dust. Their behavior communicates something that they don't intend. That doesn't mean they don't care; in fact it could even mean that they're consumed with doing something originally intended to help, but they've lost track of why they're doing it and now they're obsessed with completing the project. This certainly doesn't justify their behavior, but if you interpret it as meaning that they don't care, it will make matters worse.

One way to break this cycle is to first acknowledge their good intentions, and then be very curious: "I know that you want to do the best for us, but do you know how it makes me feel when you talk to me that way? Did you mean to make me feel bad? Does it matter to you that I feel lonely when you're away so much?" Depending on how far that gets you, you'll probably need to let them know in no uncertain terms the impact they have on you, no matter how noble their intentions.

In general, whenever you can point out to compulsives that they've done something that makes you feel good, it will be helpful. If they do let go of control, spend time with you, slow down and listen, or say something appreciative, tell them that you noticed it and that you appreciate it. That makes it more likely that they'll do it again.

Enlist their perfectionism and goal-oriented behavior in the relationship as a project. Compulsives love projects, and if the two of you can work together as a team toward a goal, it can help.

Ask for What You Need

Don't expect him or her to read your mind. He or she may be low on empathy in the first place, and may not need the same things you need. Compulsives are not naturally giving. They're obsessed with efficiency, and the intangibles such as affection just don't register unless they're alerted to the fact that other humans need them. They tend to deny their own needs and imagine that we should all be able to live without any needs. You may need to slowly educate them about matters of the heart.

Timing Is Everything

If your partner is reactive, defensive, or oversensitive, it's best not to try to have a discussion when he or she is upset. Tell him or her that you really want to work it out when you're both calmer. "Let's take a break for fifteen minutes." Or, "Let's talk about it in the morning." Generally, if there is something you need to discuss, "strike while the iron is cold." Find a time when he or she is less upset to engage. There will never be a perfect time, but if overwhelmed with fear or anger, he or she may not be able to communicate well. If you can ask what he or she needs from you, and tell what you need from him or her when you're both calm, you'll probably get a more useful response.

If you find yourself avoiding this discussion, try to feel into it and see what you're avoiding. While there are times when it's best not to engage, this could be an evasion on your part. You may need help to be able to look at your reluctance objectively.

Encouraging the Compulsive to Get Help

One of the questions I'm most frequently asked is how to get a compulsive partner to go into therapy. People who have full-blown OCPD usually don't feel that they have a problem and resist getting help. Since it can be hard to get them to go to couples' counselling or individual therapy, I'll offer some suggestions on how to communicate with them about it.

- *Find an honest and positive way to describe them.* Like everyone else, compulsives are more likely to take in a positive message than a critical one. I've found that people are much more comfortable thinking of themselves as driven, rather than compulsive. Choose your own adjective; the word you choose doesn't matter so much as long as it honestly conveys how you feel about their personality, its positive qualities and downside. With this in mind, suggest that the reason for them to seek help is not a matter of their under-functioning, but that they are driven (or whatever term you think describes them well): they've got lots of energy and they've gotten into a habit of overfunctioning. This is not a matter of weakness, but of excessive strength. Because it is such a deeply embedded pattern, they may need a professional to interrupt it.
- *Appeal to their self-interest in terms of their goals.* Point out how their control and perfectionism actually get in the way of them achieving their goals. They may also have lost sight of what they really want to achieve. Therapy can help them to reclaim and reach those goals, including self-understanding and psychological growth.
- *Appeal to their self-interest in terms of their well-being.* Point out the impact their lifestyle has on their physical and mental health. They may be oblivious to how they're treating themselves, and they could probably be healthier and happier than they are.
- *Appeal to their desire not to hurt others.* Unless there are other serious mental health issues involved, no compulsive wants to hurt

others. But they do need help in understanding how they do hurt others and how to stop. Point out that it would be helpful to you since their way of doing things has been hurtful. Working with a therapist can help them to understand the impact they have on others. Part of the therapist's job is to give them reality checks about how other people experience them. No book can convey this, only a real interaction with another human being. A trained and objective human can be especially effective.

Set Boundaries

While it is important to see the good in compulsive partners and to be mindful of how you speak to them, it's also important that you communicate that they can't treat you badly. A diagnosis of OCPD should not be used as justification for aggressive behavior or forcing you into their way of living. Don't tolerate any sort of abuse. While people with OCPD are usually not aggressive, they can explode if they haven't learned to communicate well. If they want to be perfectionistic, workaholic, or controlling that's their choice, but they should not impose their standards on you. Seek compromise that considers emotional needs for both of you, but don't give in to unrealistic demands. If they need everything to be perfect, they should get help with that.

Lilly Speaks Her Mind

Lilly was looking at Leonard differently, but the way he was treating her just wasn't OK. One night as they were getting ready to attend one of his work functions, he told her she should change her clothes, and he got angry that she was running late. After it was over, he told her she should have been more engaging and that she wasn't helping him to move up the ladder.

The next morning, when he was calmer, she said "Look Leonard, I know you want to get ahead at work and you want to buy us a house, but I just can't take this anymore. How do you think I feel being held responsible for your position at work?"

Leonard didn't know what to say. He felt defensive, but it wasn't like this was the first time he had heard this kind of thing from a woman. He really didn't want to lose Lilly, but it wasn't so easy for him to change gears. "I'm under a lot of pressure and I'm not sure you realize it."

It was really hard for Lilly to keep pushing, but she stood up for her-self, and for him, against his compulsive work and critical demeanor: "Maybe the pressure isn't worth it. What do you want this promotion for? If it's to make me happy, forget it. It's not working. If you really want me to be with you, I need you to find a way to treat me better. You may not be sensitive to this kind of thing, but I am. We're really different, and that's not bad, but if we're going to work things out, we need to find a way to make sure we're both satisfied. I'll try to meet you halfway, but I need you to change too. We've been trying to work this out for a while. I know you're trying, but I think we really need help. Besides, you haven't seemed to be happy and that's not helping you at work either."

Surprisingly, Leonard didn't balk this time. He was actually a little relieved to have her bring it up. Even though he didn't know how to express it, she meant a lot to him.

Active Self-Care

Avoid the Division of Labor

In chapter 11 I described a division of labor that relationships some-times fall into. Couples and families are self-balancing systems. What doesn't get expressed by one member of that system often gets ex-pressed by another member. This is especially true in the situation with compulsives because they're often drawn to people who are more joyful, playful, and sensitive in order to balance their work-oriented life. People who don't like to plan and organize are often attracted to people whom they experience as strong and reliable managers. This arrangement feels great at first, but it sets up inevitable problems down the road.

You might be trying the get the other person to live out your unlived life, your shadow, that part of you that doesn't get exposed to the light. The shadow isn't necessarily bad, it's just unconscious and unlived. In fact, it holds great possibility for both partners if they can claim their own shadow and develop it consciously rather than expect the other person to live it out for them.

A typical division of labor happens when one person is serious and demanding while the other is easygoing and accepting. One brings responsibility, discipline, and reason; the other brings joy, emotion, and spontaneity. If you expect your partner to do all the organizing, providing, and disciplining, don't be surprised if he or she gets very cranky, resentful, and inflexible. When compulsives are put into that role, they often get into a very rigid state of mind that's hard to relinquish. One defining characteristic of people with OCPD is a heightened sense of conscientiousness. They feel immense responsibility, whether it's realistic or not.

Imagine a spectrum from extreme compulsivity to extreme casualness. Imagine that the further one person in a pair goes toward either end, the more the other person automatically moves toward the opposite end. Now imagine that one person moves toward the center. The other will usually also move toward the center.

If you've fallen into an arrangement in which you occupy the casual end of the spectrum, it's also not fair to you: your own psychological well-being is compromised as the one who lives entirely at the less driven end of the spectrum, and you miss out on some aspects of life that could be really fulfilling. Do you allow him or her to live out your ambition for you? Do you feel uncomfortable with your own strength and anger and you let him or her express it for you? Or, on the other hand, do you express all the anger for him or her if he or she feels it's wrong to express anger?

Research has shown that people with full-blown OCPD can become irritated when the other person is being warm and sensitive.[1] They may feel that this frustrates their efforts to achieve their goals. So, staying entirely in the role of the kind, generous one may actually backfire on you anyway. While I don't recommend responding to them in the same way they treat you, improving the relationship may require you to own more of your own strength in a healthy way.

As a psychotherapist I generally encourage people to be true to themselves, and you may well be a very easygoing, kind person. But I also suspect that buried deeper within you is a part that has goals and can stand up for what you need. You might find it rewarding to allow yourself some ambition and pursue your own accomplishments. You might find it empowering to own your own anger in a constructive way. If you can resist the division of labor, it can help the compulsive to move more toward the center of the spectrum.

This division of labor can cause another problem: you're more likely to be angry at them for doing the things you don't allow yourself to do. Even if you aren't aware of it, part of you may be tired of being nice and would enjoy being a little more aggressive.

Also try to understand how your own buttons may be getting pushed. No one likes to be criticized, but you may have an amplified response to reasonable feedback if you were criticized a lot as a child, or if you were never exposed to teasing or scrutiny and never developed any tolerance for it.

Another dangerous aspect of living solely on one end of a spectrum is that you could take a victim role in response to their hostility, control, or overworking. Ask yourself honestly if there is anything you get out of the situation. Has it been safer or more comfortable to have someone else making all the plans and decisions? It may have allowed you to avoid responsibility that you'd rather not have to deal with. Or, is it gratifying to prove that you're always being abandoned? Also, for some people, tolerating egregious or hostile behavior may feel like a virtue, when it doesn't really help either of you.

Whatever your relationship is to the compulsive person in your life, it's important not to let his or her condition become the focus of your life. It could become a distraction from your own challenges and happiness. If you find yourself talking and thinking about them often, set an intention to focus on what is within your control: change either the situation or your attitude toward it.

Remember What You Offer

You may need to hold a paradox: while neither of you can live out the unlived life of the other, there are probably aspects of your personality that he or she wants and needs. Your liveliness, good cheer, consideration, support, and more relaxed style are all qualities that probably help sustain him or her. I say this partly to reinforce some of your characteristics, but also to embolden you to feel secure; he or she was attracted to you for a reason. While you can't live out parts of your partner's life, remember that you have a great deal to offer him or her.

If you've seen Jack Nicholson and Helen Hunt in the film *As Good as It Gets*, you've seen what I'm talking about. Nicholson plays a grouchy, asocial, bachelor novelist, who has both OCD and a Hollywood version of OCPD. Helen Hunt is the single mother who is his waitress at the restaurant where he eats every day. She's the only waitress who will tolerate him, and she's able to do it by setting limits on his behavior. She tries to educate him about manners, and, eventually to some degree, about matters of the heart. But perhaps the clearest message in the film is his need for her. Her waitressing is only a metaphor for the sensitivity and true self care that he so lacks and craves.

Set Up Your Own Support
In order to maintain yourself and develop your own strengths, it will help to expand your social network. Having friends, a therapist, or a support group takes pressure off the relationship and gives you a broader base for emotional sustenance. These can be especially helpful if the compulsive person in your life is demanding. A support network can help you maintain a sense not necessarily of what's right and wrong, but of what you can reasonably offer in response to your partner's needs without betraying your own needs. Ask your friends for true reality checks. If you simply want to be validated as the one who is "right," it won't be much help. But asking trusted friends for honest feedback about what you can realistically expect of yourself can help keep you grounded.

If you're unable to find this sort of support locally, you may be able to get some help from online support groups for those with OCPD that also offer support for their families. Facebook, Reddit, and Tap-A-Talk all have OCPD support groups, including groups that offer support specifically for partners of those with OCPD. These groups host message boards with resources and discussion. You can read how others have dealt with their struggles, post questions, and engage in discussion.

Lilly Rediscovers Herself
When Lilly and Leonard began couples' therapy, the therapist asked each of them to say what they loved about the other person, and what they needed from the other person that they weren't getting. To her surprise, Leonard said that he actually wished that Lilly could feel free to be more independent. He had been feeling that he needed to take care of her and that caused him more anxiety, which led to more demands and controlling behavior.

The therapist pointed out that Leonard seemed annoyed at her for trying so hard to please him. Leonard didn't want to admit this at first, but did acknowledge that there was a little truth to that. While the therapist often called Leonard on his issues, she also pointed out that Lilly had her own role in this in that she had abandoned her own life for his, and that wasn't helping. She had her own work to do, too, figuring out why she let it happen and what she could do about it.

This was all actually liberating for Lilly. She had neglected her own interests when they moved in together, trying to make the home nice for Leonard while still working at her job as a nurse. She hadn't been to the gym in eight months. She hadn't seen her friends in just as long. Her own life had been depleted, and getting her own life back was part of her work.

She was also surprised to see how much she meant to Leonard. For some reason he felt more comfortable saying it in therapy than outside.

Neither their sessions nor their lives outside of sessions were all smooth sailing after that, but there was a noticeable shift of energy. Leonard became less the center of their joint attention. The relationship itself got more attention, and Lilly focused more on her own life again. She tried to keep in mind how much pressure he felt, and to remember that that was part of what led to his rigidity. She helped him when she could do it without betraying herself. She also learned to say no.

Leonard eventually moved into a management position where his mentors helped transform his bossiness into effective and caring leadership.

Lilly entered individual therapy and began to understand that her own way of handling anxiety was to become compliant, rather than to get bossy as Leonard did. Her own insecurity made her vulnerable to feeling that she wasn't loved, when in fact she was. She began to cultivate her own self-respect and long-forgotten goals. She got involved in her own project, volunteering her nursing skills for refugees. She took back the wheel of her own life and that helped the relationship to thrive again.

~

Afterword

Looking Back

It's been four years since I began working on this book. Writing it has forced me to look at my own behavior and attitudes; I've tried to always ask myself if what I was writing was actually true in my own experience, not just according to research or clinical theory. It's been humbling to see the persistence of my patterns, but encouraging to note that I am able, with time and work, to make conscious choices to use my energy in healthy ways. I can't be objective about my own growth, but I do believe that becoming more aware of my driven nature has helped me to indulge it less and to use it more.

It's been more than twenty-five years since I began working as a therapist. I've observed that we each have our own individual religion. I'm not necessarily referring to formal creeds, denominations, stone buildings, and rituals. Rather I'm referring to a personal sense of what holds the greatest meaning for us, what we depend on, and what we prioritize, whether it's money, success, status, sex, alcohol, partners, contributing to the greater good, family, or personal growth. Most people don't consciously decide and articulate their "religion," and that's part of the problem. They tend to live according to these values automatically, without reflecting on them. But choosing and embracing truly gratifying sources of meaning consciously is necessary to live on the healthy end of the compulsive spectrum.

A related observation from my clinical experience is about what helps us to move toward that healthy end of the spectrum. The transformation is subtle, and often neither the therapist nor the patient is aware of it. But if you step back and look at the big picture of what has transpired, you can usually see that what's happened is that a faith in the process of growth has been awakened or renewed. A sense of hope, momentum, and direction emerges that helps us to navigate and steer. We've not only taken the wheel of our car and gotten a clearer sense of where we're going; we've also found meaning and inspiration in the fact that we're moving forward.

As I've thought about this issue for the last few years, I've often questioned whether I was being overly optimistic. My patients, however, have often unwittingly confirmed the important role of psychological momentum, inspiring the work that I do every day. Many of them have shown me that growing forward is what gave them the secure base from which to keep working when life became particularly difficult.

As one patient who was learning to live in a more balanced way explained to me, "It's a lot like riding a bicycle: keeping your balance is much easier when you're moving forward."

For people who are driven, becoming healthy often requires a shift of attitude, one in which we value the development of personal traits alongside those of external achievements. While using our energy to find our place in the outer world is necessary and can be fulfilling, turning that energy toward the Inner Game, in the long run, is the more satisfying and healing project. When we turn our energies to the balanced development of the personality and an orientation to inner momentum, other goals are put into their appropriate place and into their proper perspective.

It's been more than forty years since my initial fascination with psychology and spirituality first sparked my interest in knowing myself. Discoveries have continued to come since the early realizations about the Inner Game, and Self 1 and Self 2 that I mentioned in the preface. But those early themes have stayed with me: Who is this Self 2 who can help me play the Inner Game? Who or what is it inside of me that drives me? What can I learn from it? What is this drive *for*?

The Role of Healthy Compulsion in the Larger World

There is a reason that some of us are compulsive. Nature "wants" to grow and expand so that it can adapt and thrive, and it needs different sorts of people to do that. Including compulsives.

Joseph Campbell, the great twentieth-century mythologist, outlined the course of the Hero's Journey: leave home, venture into the underworld where you confront your demons, and then—and too often this is left out—then return to your village to share the boon that you discovered.

This is why advocating the Inner Game is not a selfish approach to life, rather that we discover and develop who we are so that we can be more fulfilled and be of service to our community. As all people do, no matter what their personality type, people who are driven have an important place in the world. We tend to make things happen—for better or worse. We are catalysts. Nature has given us this drive; how will we use it? Finding that role and living it consciously solves the riddle I raised in the introduction: what are these compulsive urges for? Finding and living our unique, individual role, no matter how small or insignificant it seems, is the most healing action we can take.

However, we can only determine that role to a limited degree. When Self 1 doesn't accept this, we become unhealthy.

Sharing the Reins

I've often wondered if the subtitle and metaphor for this book, "Taking the Wheel of the Driven Personality," would mislead my readers. It's really about sharing control—not taking it.

"Taking the wheel" is a modern version of the ancient archetypal image of the charioteer taking the reins of his chariot. He looks heroic and determined. In control. In fact, Carl Jung said that he would never want to be a charioteer because he'd rather not be in control—he preferred the creativity that Self 2, the unconscious, has to offer to the certainty that Self 1, the ego, offers.[1]

But I think that the best charioteers actually take their directions from Self 2. They hold the reins, but the soul charts the course. That was clearly the case with the hero of Indian mythology, Arjuna, one of the greatest archers of all time. Watching the battle from his chariot, he realized that Krishna, his soul, was really his guide. The outcome of the battle was not his to decide. He held the reins, but he was not in control of them.

The fact that I'm saying this may make you suspicious. Why shouldn't you be? There is no little man or woman inside of us pulling the levers. But an increasing amount of research indicates that there is wisdom to be gained from the unconscious[2]—if we can let go enough to trust it. All those different parts of the personality I've been referring to in this book contribute to this wisdom to the degree that they are recognized and respected, and to the degree that they work together cooperatively. These personality parts often show up in our dreams as threatening or in desperate need of help. These are the characters that produce the urges we call compulsions. Collectively they constitute the guidance that Self 2 has to offer.

I've been tempted to subtitle this book "Turning Over the Wheel of the Driven Personality" because in the end it's not an act of will, or more powerful control by the ego that leads to a healthier life; rather, it's a letting go and turning it over to those original passions that really motivated our first urges. Or, more accurately, a partial letting go and turning over.

I kept the subtitle "Taking Over the Wheel," partly because most of us are not emotionally ready to turn over the wheel at first, and because we do first need to take it back from the frightened parts of us that have hijacked our talents. But also because even when we eventually drive in service of a more meaningful direction, it's a collaborative effort between Self 1 (the executive function, the ego) and Self 2 (the soul that gives meaning and direction).

That is the heroic task of the healthy compulsive—to maintain control of the wheel while still being open to input from Self 2 or the unconscious. My hope is that this book will help us all in this balancing act and that we will all benefit from this drive we call compulsion.

~

Acknowledgments

Many friends and colleagues have generously given their time, sugges-tions, and support in the years that this book has taken shape. Thanks to Michael Dowling, Nancy Eisenman, Kathryn Staley, and Nancy Ulrich for reading early drafts of the book and giving encouragement and feedback. My time with Charles Salzberg and the New York Writers Workshop was indispensable in shaping the book and its tone. Thanks to Steve Harris at CSG Literary Partners for finding a home for *The Healthy Compulsive* and for helping me navigate the world of publishing, and to Suzanne Staszak-Silva at Rowman & Littlefield for seeing the potential in the book and her patient and encouraging assistance in the final stages. Production editors Andrew Unger and Lisa Whittington saved me from many literary and scholarly embarrassments. Janet Care-swell and Gerry Compas at The C. G. Jung Foundation of New York provided support for my first book and gave me a platform to present and develop my thinking. Lorna Peachin at the Kristine Mann Library has provided friendly and knowledgeable help in research. Thanks also to all of my colleagues at the New York Association for Analytical Psychology and the C. G. Jung Institute of New York for their support and confidence.

The "ten thousand" (and counting) interactions with friends at the Cedar Knolls Zen Sangha and the First Unitarian Society of Westchester have helped me stay sane and inspired me to walk consciously, communally, and joyfully on this precious Earth.

Once again, thanks to Nancy, Zoe, and Thea for their love and patience, and for reminding me of what's most important. But most of all for simply being who they are.

~

Notes

Preface

1. W. Timothy Gallwey, *The Inner Game of Tennis* (New York: Random House, 1974).

2. C. G. Jung and S. Shamdasani, eds., *The Red Book: Liber Novus*, trans. M. Kyburz and J. Peck (New York: Norton, 2009), 277.

3. "The urge and compulsion to self-realization is a law of nature and thus of invincible power" (C. G. Jung, "The Psychology of the Child Archetype," in *The Collected Works of C. G. Jung*, vol. 9.1 [Princeton: Bollingen, 1959], para. 289).

Introduction

1. In *America's Obsessives: The Compulsive Energy That Built a Nation* (New York: Grand Central Publishing, 2013) author Joshua Kendall describes Steve Jobs, Melvil Dewey, Thomas Jefferson, Ted Williams, Alfred Kinsey, Estee Lauder, and Charles Lindbergh all as being compulsive. In each case, there were healthy and unhealthy aspects to their behavior.

2. Khaled Hosseini, "Author Khaled Hosseini on *The Kite Runner*," interview by Rachel Sandor, *Rotten Tomatoes*, December 5, 2007, https://editorial.rottentomatoes.com/article/author-khaled-hosseini-on-the-kite-runner-the-rt-interview/.

Chapter 1: Identifying the Driven Personality

1. Jon E. Grant, Marc E. Mooney, and Matt G. Kushner, "Prevalence, Correlates, and Comorbidity of DSM-IV Obsessive-Compulsive Personality Disorder: Results from the National Epidemiologic Survey on Alcohol and Related Conditions," *Journal of Psychiatric Research* 46, no. 4 (2012).

2. American Psychiatric Association, *Diagnostic and Statistical Manual of Mental Disorders*, 5th ed. [*DSM-5*] (Arlington, VA: American Psychiatric Publishing, 2013).

3. G. Diaconu and G. Turecki, "Obsessive-Compulsive Personality Disorder and Suicidal Behavior: Evidence for a Positive Association in a Sample of Depressed Patients," *Journal of Clinical Psychiatry* 70, no. 11 (2009).

4. Wilhelm Reich, *Character-Analysis*, 3rd, enl. ed. (New York: Orgone Institute Press, 1949).

5. K. A. Halmi et al., "The Relation among Perfectionism, Obsessive-Compulsive Personality Disorder and Obsessive-Compulsive Disorder in Individuals with Eating Disorders," *International Journal of Eating Disorders* 38, no. 4 (2005).

6. Current research efforts to understand OCPD are using a dimensional model of personality traits, viewing them on a spectrum rather than through a categorical (yes or no) model. The idea is that diagnostic categories such as OCPD represent maladaptive variants of *general* personality traits, traits that otherwise are healthy. Using a dimensional model, people are understood to behave on a scale of healthy to unhealthy in regard to categories such as conscientiousness, persistence, and achievement. Healthy compulsives utilize these characteristics well, whereas unhealthy compulsives become slaves to them. D. B. Samuel and T. A. Widiger, "Conscientiousness and Obsessive-Compulsive Personality Disorder," *Personality Disorders: Theory, Research, and Treatment* 2, no. 3 (2011); T. A. Widiger and G. T. Smith, "Personality and Psychopathology," in *Handbook of Personality: Theory and Research*, ed. O. P. John, R. W. Robins, and L. A. Pervin (New York: Guilford Press, 2008); C. Crego, D. B. Samuel, and T. A. Widiger, "The FFOCI and Other Measures and Models of OCPD," *Assessment* 22, no. 2 (2015).

7. Even people with OCPD can have strengths that are a result of their basic disposition. Just as one example of how this can work, subjects with OCPD were found to have better visual perception than those who didn't have OCPD. An unhealthy compulsive might get lost in the details, but they might also notice dangers or possibilities that others would not. While people who are not compulsive might miss the beauty of individual trees but find it easier to appreciate the large view of the forest, compulsives may miss the forest but

can appreciate the tiniest details of nature that others don't notice. Zohreh Ansari and Javad Salehi Fadardi, "Enhanced Visual Performance in Obsessive Compulsive Personality Disorder," *Scandinavian Journal of Psychology* 57, no. 6 (2016).

8. Only about 20 percent of the people who have OCPD also have OCD. Maria C. Mancebo, Jane L. Eisen, Jon E. Grant, and Steven A. Rasmussen, "Obsessive Compulsive Personality Disorder and Obsessive Compulsive Disorder: Clinical Characteristics, Diagnostic Difficulties, and Treatment," *Annals of Clinical Psychiatry* 17, no. 4 (2005).

9. A. Pinto, J. E. Steinglass, A. L. Greene, E. U. Weber, and H. B. Simpson, "Capacity to Delay Reward Differentiates Obsessive-Compulsive Disorder and Obsessive-Compulsive Personality Disorder," *Biological Psychiatry* 75, no. 8 (2014).

10. N. M. Cain, E. B. Ansell, H. B. Simpson, and A. Pinto, "Interpersonal Functioning in Obsessive-Compulsive Personality Disorder," *Journal of Personality Assessment* 97, no. 1 (2015).

11. Leonard Cammer, *Freedom from Compulsion: How to Liberate Yourself from the Uptight, Obsessive Patterns of Living That Rob You of Peace of Mind* (New York: Simon and Schuster, 1976).

Chapter 2: How Did I Get This Way?

1. There certainly is no one gene that determines your personality style. Rather it seems to be the result of a collection of genes that are expressed to varying degrees. Alice Diedrich of the Ludwig Maximilian University of Munich writes: "Some of the few studies that have been conducted in individuals with OCPD indicate associations between OCPD and the dopamine D3 receptor Gly/Gly genotype, the serotonin transporter 5HTTLPR polymorphism, and a blunted prolactin response to fenfluramine indicating a potential serotonergic dysfunction." If you understand all that, it's a good thing you're reading this book. Those of you who do understand it know that this means that while the good folks in research labs working on this still have a ways to go, we do have strong indications that aspects of a compulsive style are genetic. A. Diedrich and U. Voderholzer, "Obsessive-Compulsive Personality Disorder: A Current Review," *Current Psychiatry Reports* 17, no. 2 (2015).

2. Identical twins who were raised apart tend to score similarly on scales of compulsivity, indicating that their parenting and environment only partly determined their personality. Let's say that you were born an identical twin, that is, you have the exact same genetic material as the kid you roomed with *in utero*. But for some reason your parents weren't able to raise the two of you,

so you and your twin were adopted by different families. The research we have indicates that if one of you has OCPD tendencies the other is likely to have them also, even if you were raised in different environments. So even if your brother got the family with the spick-and-span mansion and you got the one with the filthy shack, you'll probably score similarly on an OCPD scale.

If you were born a fraternal twin, that is, if you and your twin share only 50 percent of your genetic load, the chances are half as good that you'll both be compulsive. L. C. Gjerde et al., "A Longitudinal, Population-Based Twin Study of Avoidant and Obsessive-Compulsive Personality Disorder Traits from Early to Middle Adulthood," *Psychological Medicine* 45, no. 16 (2015); S. Torgersen et al., "A Twin Study of Personality Disorders," *Comprehensive Psychiatry* 41, no. 6 (2000); D. S. van Grootheest, M. Bartels, C. E. van Beijsterveldt, D. C. Cath, A. T. Beekman, J. J. Hudziak, and D. I. Boomsma, "Genetic and Environmental Contributions to Self-Report Obsessive-Compulsive Symptoms in Dutch Adolescents at Ages 12, 14, and 16," *Journal of the American Academy of Child and Adolescent Psychiatry* 47, no. 10 (2008); Christine Clifford, Robin Murray, and D. W. Fulker, "Genetic and Environmental Influences on Obsessional Traits and Symptoms," *Psychological Medicine* 14, no. 4 (1984): 791–800.

Back in the late 1990s some scientists in Sweden wanted to sort out this nature-versus-nurture controversy in regard to Type A personality, a personality type characterized by a sense of urgency and competitiveness. Lucky for the researchers, the Swedes have a national registry of twins and adoptees that allowed them to measure which had more effect, genes or environment. So they studied identical twins raised in the same home and identical twins who were adopted and raised apart. They also studied fraternal twins raised together, and fraternal twins who were raised apart. Their data indicates that genes account for more of our personality than the way we were raised—but only regarding certain aspects of the unhealthy profile.

What's really interesting about this study is that they were able to consider whether certain characteristics of type A's were more genetically determined or environmental. It turns out that some aspects of Type A personality, for example being pressured, hard-driving, and ambitious, were more likely to be inherited, while other aspects, specifically hostility and assertion, were determined more by environment and family. So, you can be born with the propensity to be driven, but just how cooperative or belligerent you become to reach your goals is shaped more by your environment than by your genes. Nancy L. Pedersen et al., "Genetic and Environmental Influences for Type A-Like Measures and Related Traits: A Study of Twins Reared Apart and Twins Reared Together," *Psychosomatic Medicine* 51 (1989).

3. B. Hummelen, T. Wilberg, G. Pedersen, and S. Karterud, "The Quality of the DSM-IV Obsessive-Compulsive Personality Disorder Construct as a Prototype Category," *Journal of Nervous and Mental Disease* 196, no. 6 (2008).

4. Zohreh Ansari and Javad Salehi Fadardi, "Enhanced Visual Performance in Obsessive Compulsive Personality Disorder," *Scandinavian Journal of Psychology* 57, no. 6 (2016).

5. Pedersen et al., "Genetic and Environmental Influences."

6. Melinda Beck, "Inside the Minds of the Perfectionists: Researchers Used to Blame Parenting but Studies Suggest a Genetic Link; Procrastination Is a Problem," *Wall Street Journal*, October 29, 2012; C. Iranzo-Tatay et al., "Genetic and Environmental Contributions to Perfectionism and Its Common Factors," *Psychiatry Research* 230, no. 3 (2015).

7. E. J. Connolly and K. M. Beaver, "Examining the Genetic and Environmental Influences on Self-Control and Delinquency: Results from a Genetically Informative Analysis of Sibling Pairs," *Journal of Interpersonal Violence* 29, no. 4 (2014).

8. Kaili Rimfeld, Yulia Kovas, Philip S. Dale, and Robert Plomin, "True Grit and Genetics: Predicting Academic Achievement from Personality," *Journal of Personality and Social Psychology* 111, no. 5 (2016).

9. George A. Morgan, Robert J. Harmon, and Christine Maslin-Cole, "Mastery Motivation: Definition and Measurement," *Early Education and Development* 1, no. 5 (1990). Morgan and his colleagues defined mastery motivation as "a psychological force that stimulates an individual to independently, in a focused and persistent manner, solve a problem or master a skill or task which is at least moderately challenging for him or her." Their research led them to believe that the characteristic is partly genetic.

10. While Panksepp was not specific about a possible link between compulsive personality style and what he called seeking behavior, his emphasis on the biological roots of motivations, emotion and behavior, certainly imply a genetic root for it, both in its normal manifestations and pathological variants. J. Panksepp, "Emotional Endophenotypes in Evolutionary Psychiatry," *Progress in Neuro-Psychopharmacology and Biological Psychiatry* 30, no. 5 (2006).

For a clear explanation of Panksepp's work on seeking, see Sara-Neena Koch's blog at http://mybrainnotes.com/brain-ocd-dopamine.html.

11. S. I. Di Domenico and R. M. Ryan, "The Emerging Neuroscience of Intrinsic Motivation: A New Frontier in Self-Determination Research," *Frontiers in Human Neuroscience* 11 (2017): 145.

12. People who are driven are more likely to find pleasure in challenging experiences, also known as "flow." Recent research indicates that those people who are more likely to experience flow have more capability to receive dopamine as

a result of these experiences. O. de Manzano et al., "Individual Differences in the Proneness to Have Flow Experiences Are Linked to Dopamine D2-Receptor Availability in the Dorsal Striatum," *Neuroimage* 67 (2013); M. Gyurkovics et al., "Individual Differences in Flow Proneness Are Linked to a Dopamine D2 Receptor Gene Variant," *Consciousness and Cognition* 42 (2016).

13. K. L. Jang, W. J. Livesley, and P. A. Vernon, "Heritability of the Big Five Personality Dimensions and Their Facets: A Twin Study," *Journal of Personality* 64, no. 3 (1996).

14. Itamar Simonson and Aner Sela, "On the Heritability of Consumer Decision Making: An Exploratory Approach for Studying Genetic Effects on Judgment and Choice," *Journal of Consumer Research* 37, no. 6 (2011)."Consistent with dictionary definitions of prudence, as used here, the term can encompass aspects such as cautiousness, carefulness, discretion, moderation, being mindful, and being prepared."

15. "When we accuse others of laziness or stinginess, we are driven by something deeper and hotter than sheer reason—by a feeling of moral indignation, of just grievance. And the feeling—found in cultures everywhere—seems to be grounded in our genes. According to evolutionary psychologists, it is part of the emotional equipment designed by natural selection to govern reciprocal altruism, to help us play non-zero sum games profitably" (Robert Wright, *Nonzero: The Logic of Human Destiny* [New York: Pantheon Books, 2000], 29).

16. It seems that parents who are rigid themselves and discourage flexibility and spontaneity contribute to an unhealthy compulsive style. We do have research that indicates that many who suffer from OCPD had fathers, at least, who were critical and perfectionistic. Randy O. Frost, Gail Steketee, Leslie Cohn, and Kristine Griess, "Personality Traits in Subclinical and Non-Obsessive-Compulsive Volunteers and Their Parents," *Behaviour Research and Therapy* 32, no. 1 (1994): 47–56.

Other studies indicate that critical mothers often raise pathologically perfectionistic daughters. Roz Shafran and Warren Mansell, "Perfectionism and Psychopathology: A Review of Research and Treatment," *Clinical Psychology Review* 21, no. 6 (2001); Hans M. Nordahl and Tore Stiles, "Perceptions of Parental Bonding in Patients with Various Personality Disorders, Lifetime Depressive Disorders, and Healthy Controls," *Journal of Personality Disorders* 11, no. 4 (1997).

17. Frost et al., "Personality Traits."

18. N. Kulish, "Precocious Ego Development and Obsessive Compulsive Neurosis," *Journal of American Academy of Psychoanalysis* 16, no. 2 (1988).

19. Nordahl and Stiles, "Perceptions of Parental Bonding."

20. Given a different experience and other choices, driven people may choose a different lifestyle. Interestingly, in the eighteenth century, when

white Europeans with their protestant work ethics were captured by Native Americans, they never went back to their supposedly virtuous and more civilized families. Native Americans, on the other hand, always went back. I wonder why. While this is pure speculation, perhaps they realized how maladjusted the whole world of the white Anglo-Saxon protestant was. Perhaps those of us caught in commercial culture are also in a sort of trance. We are so surrounded by it that we can't see it. David Brooks, "The Great Affluence Fallacy," *New York Times*, August 9, 2016.

21. Andrew J. Elliot and Marcy A. Church, "A Hierarchical Model of Approach and Avoidance Achievement Motivation," *Journal of Personality and Social Psychology* 72, no. 1 (1997). One way that this has been described in the research literature is as the difference between approach behavior and avoidance behavior. Approach behavior has been found to be both more fulfilling and more successful. Edward L. Deci and Richard M. Ryan, "The 'What' and 'Why' of Goal Pursuits: Human Needs and the Self-Determination of Behavior," *Psychological Inquiry* 11, no. 4 (2000): 227–68. It is also known as intrinsic motivation, as opposed to extrinsic, intrinsic motivation being recognized as more effective in helping people to reach their goals. Di Domenico and Ryan, "Emerging Neuroscience of Intrinsic Motivation."

22. Sigmund Freud, the father of psychoanalysis, believed that some children who were born with certain sensitivities and raised by controlling parents were inclined to develop unhealthy compulsivity. He believed that they had been born with anal sensitivity, and the controlling parent part came along during toilet training. As a result, the child became orderly, parsimonious, and obstinate. To be graphic, some children would hold onto their feces in order to control the parents, to extract revenge for their parents' attempts to control them, but at the same time without getting in trouble. Thus the description: he's really "anal."

The specific anal and toilet training parts, it turns out, have no support. However, as was often the case, Freud was onto something, but couldn't quite put his finger on exactly what was happening. Essentially he was saying that the bases for the compulsive personality are the fit between the child's constitutional style and his or her controlling parents, and, most importantly, the child's reaction, how he dealt with the fit between the two. The child becomes angry at his parents, but, because he is afraid of them and unable to express his anger directly, he punishes them with passive-aggressive behavior. In an additional effort to keep his anger from offending his parents, he becomes hypercontrolling of himself. There is something symbolically accurate about this; we become afraid of the crap that we'll let out and so we hold it in; we become determined to be clean and orderly. In effect we become afraid of our own impulses.

23. Rob J. M. Reus and Paul M. G. Emmelkamp, "Obsessive–Compulsive Personality Disorder: A Review of Current Empirical Findings," *Personality and Mental Health* 6, no. 1 (2012).

24. Ibid.; D. P. Devanand et al., "Personality Disorders in Elderly Patients with Dysthymic Disorder," *American Journal of Geriatric Psychiatry* 8, no. 3 (2000).

25. George H. Weinberg, *Invisible Masters: Compulsions and the Fear That Drives Them* (New York: Grove Press, 1993), 89.

26. J. E. Grant, M. N. Potenza, A. Weinstein, and D. A. Gorelick, "Introduction to Behavioral Addictions," *American Journal of Drug and Alcohol Abuse* 36, no. 5 (2010): 233–41.

27. Pier Vincenzo Piazza and Michel Le Moal, "Glucocorticoids as a Biological Substrate of Reward: Physiological and Pathophysiological Implications," *Brain Research Reviews* 25, no. 3 (1997), 359–72.

Chapter 3: Four Steps to Becoming a Healthier Compulsive

1. As with research regarding the cause of OCPD, research regarding the treatment of it is still in its early stages. Nevertheless, we do have data that indicate that many types of therapy (including cognitive therapy, cognitive behavioral therapy, dialectical behavioral therapy, behavioral therapy, schema therapy, interpersonal therapy, and supportive expressive therapy) can all be effective. A. Diedrich and U. Voderholzer, "Obsessive-Compulsive Personality Disorder: A Current Review," *Current Psychiatry Reports* 17, no. 2 (2015): 2, doi: 10.1007/s11920-014-0547-8; J. P. Barber, "Change in Obsessive-Compulsive and Avoidant Personality Disorders Following Time-Limited Supportive Expressive Therapy," *Psychotherapy* 34, no. 2 (1997); J. P. Barber and L. R. Muenz, "The Role of Avoidance and Obsessiveness in Matching Patients to Cognitive and Interpersonal Psychotherapy: Empirical Findings from the Treatment for Depression Collaborative Research Program," *Journal of Consulting and Clinical Psychology* 64, no. 5 (1996): 951–58.

Chapter 4: Step 1: Identify Your Story to Develop Insight

1. Edward O. Wilson, *The Meaning of Human Existence* (New York: Liveright Publishing Corporation, a division of W.W. Norton & Company, 2014), 15.

2. The language of Parent, Adult, and Child is borrowed from Transactional Analysis. See Thomas Anthony Harris, *I'm Ok, You're Ok; A Practical Guide to Transactional Analysis* (New York: Harper & Row, 1969).

3. Eric Weiner, *The Geography of Bliss: One Grump's Search for the Happiest Places in the World* (New York: Twelve/Hachette, 2008), 139–40.

Chapter 5: Step 2: Engage Emotionally with Deeper Layers of Feeling and Parts of Yourself

1. Richard Pimentel, a Vietnam veteran who lost his hearing during the war, was a prominent figure in the passage of the Americans with Disabilities Act. His story is documented in the film *The Music Within*. He was born driven. He had a talent for public speaking and a passion for doing the right thing. Despite horrendous childhood conditions, he used his abilities for the greater good—eventually. It was not an easy road. Richard struggled with alcoholism and destroyed a relationship with his workaholic tendencies. He lost the capacity to savor his work when he became driven by his anger. Once he realized this, he was able to return to the original reasons he loved his work and the meaning and purpose behind it. He then went on to a very fulfilling career.

2. According to research regarding people with OCPD conducted by psychologists Michael Wheaton and Anthony Pinto, the more unwilling they are to experience their unpleasant emotions, thoughts, and sensations, and the more they try to avoid them, the worse their compulsive symptoms are. Their emotions are actually amplified, and their behavior gets worse. The researchers concluded that individuals with OCPD should learn to accept and tolerate their emotions. Michael G. Wheaton and Anthony Pinto, "The Role of Experiential Avoidance in Obsessive–Compulsive Personality Disorder Traits," *Personality Disorders: Theory, Research, and Treatment* 8, no. 4 (2017): 383–88.

As a result of their research, Maria Steenkamp and her colleagues reported: "Participants with OCPD reported significantly higher levels of negative affectivity, trait anger, emotional intensity, and emotion regulation difficulties. Emotion regulation difficulties included lack of emotional clarity, nonacceptance of emotional responses, and limited access to effective emotion regulation strategies" (Maria M. Steenkamp, Michael K. Suvak, Benjamin D. Dickstein, M. Tracie Shea, and Brett T. Litz, "Emotional Functioning in Obsessive-Compulsive Personality Disorder: Comparison to Borderline Personality Disorder and Healthy Controls," *Journal of Personality Disorders* 29, no. 6 [2015]).

3. James W. Pennebaker, and Janel D. Seagal, "Forming a Story: The Health Benefits of Narrative," *Journal of Clinical Psychology* 55, no. 10 (1999):

1243–54; Michael White and David Epston, *Narrative Means to Therapeutic Ends* (New York: Norton, 1990); Karen A. Baikie and Kay Wilhelm, "Emotional and Physical Health Benefits of Expressive Writing," *Advances in Psychiatric Treatment* 11, no. 5 (2005): 338–46; Gillie Bolton, *The Therapeutic Potential of Creative Writing: Writing Myself* (Philadelphia: Jessica Kingsley, 1999).

4. Eugene Gendlin, *Focusing*, 2nd ed. (New York: Bantam, 1982).

5. Nicole R. Villemarette-Pittman et al., "Obsessive-Compulsive Personality Disorder and Behavioral Disinhibition," *Journal of Psychology* 138, no. 1 (2004).

6. Jonathan Rottenberg, *The Depths: The Evolutionary Origins of the Depression Epidemic* (New York: Basic Books, 2014).

7. Daniel Todd Gilbert, *Stumbling on Happiness* (New York: Knopf, 2006).

8. Antonio R. Damasio, *Descartes' Error: Emotion, Reason, and the Human Brain* (London: Penguin, 2005).

9. Richard Schwartz developed a method of psychotherapy called Internal Family Systems, which encourages dialogue with different parts of the personality and has been shown to improve both physical and emotional functioning, reducing physical pain and depression, and is considered an evidence-based practice. Nancy A. Shadick et al., "A Randomized Controlled Trial of an Internal Family Systems-Based Psychotherapeutic Intervention on Outcomes in Rheumatoid Arthritis: A Proof-of-Concept Study," *Journal of Rheumatology* 40, no. 11 (2013).

Internal Family Systems work is quite similar to Carl Jung's method of active imagination described by Robert A. Johnson in his book *Inner Work* (San Francisco: Harper and Row, 1986).

Chapter 6: Step 3: Cultivate Meaning

1. As psychologist Stephen Johnson has pointed out, "These individuals are known for their tendency to miss what is most important by concentrating on minor details" (*Character Styles* [New York: Norton, 1994], 277).

2. George H. Weinberg, *Invisible Masters: Compulsions and the Fear That Drives Them* (New York: Grove Press, 1993); Theodore Millon, *Disorders of Personality: DSM-III, Axis II* (New York: Wiley, 1981).

3. C. G. Jung, "Some Crucial Points in Psychoanalysis," in *Freud and Psychoanalysis*, ed. Edith Eder (New York: Bollingen, 1916), para. 669.

4. J. P. Barber, "Change in Obsessive-Compulsive and Avoidant Personality Disorders Following Time-Limited Supportive Expressive Therapy," *Psychotherapy* 34, no. 2 (1997).

Chapter 7: Step 4: Take Action

1. M. D. Griffiths and M. Karanika-Murray, "Contextualising Over-Engagement in Work: Towards a More Global Understanding of Workaholism as an Addiction," *Journal of Behavioral Addictions* 1, no. 3 (2012).

Chapter 8: Body

1. K. A. Matthews, "Matters of the Heart: Advancing Psychological Perspectives on Cardiovascular Diseases," *Perspectives on Psychological Science* 8, no. 6 (2013).

2. Bonnie Berkowitz and Clark Patterson, "The Health Hazards of Sitting," *Washington Post*, January 20, 2014.

3. Nancy McWilliams, *Psychoanalytic Diagnosis: Understanding Personality Structure in the Clinical Process*, 2nd ed. (New York: Guilford Press, 2011).

Chapter 9: Time and Money

1. Itamar Simonson and Aner Sela, "On the Heritability of Consumer Decision Making: An Exploratory Approach for Studying Genetic Effects on Judgment and Choice," *Journal of Consumer Research* 37, no. 6 (2011): 951–66.

Chapter 10: Work and Career

1. Edward L. Deci and Richard M. Ryan, "The 'What' and 'Why' of Goal Pursuits: Human Needs and the Self-Determination of Behavior," *Psychological Inquiry* 11, no. 4 (2000). Psychologists Deci and Ryan propose that humans have three basic needs: competence, relatedness, and autonomy, all necessary for psychological growth, integrity, and well-being. Compulsives probably have a greater need for competence and autonomy and may sacrifice relatedness to achieve them.

2. Neuroscientist Jaak Panksepp has found neurological networks for a primary emotion he refers to as seeking, which he understands to be an intense desire for learning, exploration, problem solving, anticipation, and accomplishment, all instrumental in survival, and therefore deeply imprinted in our biological makeup. When this primary emotion is blocked, the regular release of dopamine reward system is inhibited, and we become depressed. J. Panksepp, "Affective Neuroscience of the Emotional Brainmind: Evolutionary Perspectives and Implications for Understanding Depression," *Dialogues in Clinical Neuroscience* 12, no. 4 (2010): 533–45.

3. M. D. Griffiths, "Workaholism Is Still a Useful Construct," *Addiction Research and Theory* 13 (2005).

4. M. D. Griffiths, "A 'Components' Model of Addiction within a Biopsychosocial Framework," *Journal of Substance Use* 10 (2005).

5. C. S. Andreassen, M. D. Griffiths, J. Hetland, and S. Pallesen. "Development of a Work Addiction Scale." *Scandinavian Journal of Psychology* 53, no. 3 (2012): 265–72. Used with permission.

6. C. S. Andreassen, "Workaholism: An Overview and Current Status of the Research," *Journal of Behavioral Addictions* 3, no. 1 (2014): 1–11.

7. S. I. Di Domenico and R. M. Ryan, "The Emerging Neuroscience of Intrinsic Motivation: A New Frontier in Self-Determination Research," *Frontiers in Human Neuroscience* 11 (2017): 145. In this article the authors review "converging evidence suggesting that intrinsically motivated exploratory and mastery behaviors are phylogenetically ancient tendencies that are subserved by dopaminergic systems."

8. Christina Maslach, Wilmar B. Schaufeli, and Michael P. Leiter, "Job Burnout," *Annual Review of Psychology* 52 (2001).

9. D. W. Holland, "Work Addiction: Costs and Solutions for Individuals, Relationships and Organizations," *Journal of Workplace Behavioral Health* 22, no. 4 (2008): 1–15.

10. Christopher Orpen, "Type A Personality as a Moderator of the Effects of Role Conflict, Role Ambiguity and Role Overload on Individual Strain," *Journal of Human Stress* 8, no. 2 (1982); R. D. Caplan and K. W. Jones, "Effects of Work Load, Role Ambiguity, and Type A Personality on Anxiety, Depression, and Heart Rate," *Journal of Applied Psychology* 60, no. 6 (1975).

Chapter 11: People, Partners, and Parenting

1. A team of researchers at the University Hospital of Oslo suggests that the core pathology of OCPD includes perfectionism, rigidity, and aggression that lead to difficulties in interactions with others. They believe that these core features of OCPD might be due to their preferred use of an evolutionary adaptation known as the systemizing mechanism, the capacity to analyze and understand lawful events. This can be quite helpful, but without its corresponding and balancing mechanism, empathizing, which understands human intention, it can lead to rigidity, stubbornness, and perfectionism. They argue that OCPD develops out of an inborn tendency toward systemizing. For example, if an individual with OCPD experiences a significant other as unpredictable or not following the "rules," then he or she might experience frustration, irritability, or even rage because he or she searches for lawful patterns without understanding the human

component. B. Hummelen, T. Wilberg, G. Pedersen, and S. Karterud, "The Quality of the *DSM-IV* Obsessive-Compulsive Personality Disorder Construct as a Prototype Category," *Journal of Nervous and Mental Disease* 196, no. 6 (2008). If we understand this need to predict the behavior of others and resulting hostility in terms of determination and control gone awry, we can understand the possibility that aggressiveness is a side effect of blocked goal-directed behavior. Researcher Nicole Cain and her colleagues reported "We also found that individuals with OCPD might be able to experience empathic concern for others, but lack the skills to appropriately respond to or fully understand the affective experience of another person (low perspective taking). Treatment interventions aimed at increasing perspective taking and the capacity to respond to emotion in a fluid and appropriate manner could improve treatment outcome for this population." N. M. Cain, E. B. Ansell, H. B. Simpson, and A. Pinto, "Interpersonal Functioning in Obsessive-Compulsive Personality Disorder," *Journal of Personality Assessment* 97, no. 1 (2015).

2. Liz Mineo, "Good Genes Are Nice, but Joy Is Better," *Harvard Gazette*, April 2017, https://news.harvard.edu/gazette/story/2017/04/over-nearly-80-years-harvard-study-has-been-showing-how-to-live-a-healthy-and-happy-life. This study is flawed in that the subjects are strictly male. Yet tellingly, it supports values that are traditionally feminine.

3. Psychologist Vicki Helgeson at Carnegie Mellon University set out to find out how gender roles affect health. What she discovered was that while men in the United States tend to have more agency and die earlier, women tend to have more community but get sick more often. But she also points out that these tendencies are just that, only tendencies. Once men and women are freed from gender roles, they can espouse either agency, communion, or both. She concluded, "Both are required for optimal well-being; when one exists in the absence of the other (unmitigated communion or unmitigated agency), however, negative health outcomes occur." Unmitigated agency can kill you. Literally. It seems that the stress this causes is one of the reasons that men (who tend toward agency rather than communion) tend to die earlier than women. They tend not to develop social networks and this leaves them vulnerable to the sort of stress that causes heart attacks. Vicki S. Helgeson, "Relation of Agency and Communion to Well-Being: Evidence and Potential Explanations," *Psychological Bulletin* 116, no. 3 (1994): 412–28.

Note, too, that the earliest primates took a huge evolutionary step when they achieved this division of labor: some went out foraging (agency) while others stayed at the campsite to nest (communal). While this had its advantages, both these roles continue to operate in us, and, I would argue, constitute one of the most common conflicts within us.

4. For a beautiful example of how the good intentions of others are experienced as mean-spirited by others, read the novel *A Man Called Ove* by Fredrik Backman (New York: Washington Square Press, 2015), or watch the movie of the same name. You can read my review at http://thehealthycompulsive.com/film-review -a-man-called-ove-the-beauty-and-tragedy-of-the-compulsive-personality.

5. Amy Ellis Nutt with Frances E. Jensen, *The Teenage Brain: A Neuroscientist's Survival Guide to Raising Adolescents and Young Adults* (New York: HarperCollins, 2015).

6. Elizabeth Thompson Gershoff, "Corporal Punishment by Parents and Associated Child Behaviors and Experiences: A Meta-Analytic and Theoretical Review," *Psychological Bulletin* 128, no. 4 (2002).

Chapter 12: Rest and Play

1. Alex Soojung-Kim Pang, *Rest: Why You Get More Done When You Work Less* (New York: Basic Books, 2016).

2. Ap Dijksterhuis, "Think Different: The Merits of Unconscious Thought in Preference Development and Decision Making," *Journal of Personality and Social Psychology* 87, no. 5 (2004).

3. J. Smallwood and J. Andrews-Hanna, "Not All Minds That Wander Are Lost: The Importance of a Balanced Perspective on the Mind-Wandering State," *Frontiers in Psychology* 4 (2013); Michael C. Corballis, *The Wandering Mind: What the Brain Does When You're Not Looking* (Chicago: University of Chicago Press, 2015).

4. S. G. Shamay-Tsoory, N. Adler, J. Aharon-Peretz, D. Perry, and N. Mayseless, "The Origins of Originality: The Neural Bases of Creative Thinking and Originality," *Neuropsychologia* 49, no. 2 (2011).

5. Stuart Brown and Christopher Vaughan, *Play: How It Shapes the Brain, Opens the Imagination, and Invigorates the Soul* (New York: Penguin, 2010).

Chapter 13: Psychological Growth

1. A. H. Maslow, "A Theory of Human Motivation," *Psychological Review* 50 (1943): 370–96. Abraham Maslow suggested that self-actualization is the highest in a hierarchy of five personal needs, and that once the other needs (physiological, security, competence, and self-esteem) were met, then one could embark on self-actualization.

2. Carl Jung believed that for many, the most powerful urge, the motivation that drives us the most, is the urge to develop our own personality; he called

this instinct individuation. When he wrote "At a higher cultural level we must forgo compulsion and turn to self-development," he was encouraging us to not just "tame" the psyche, but to nurture the instinct to develop it. For while it is important to develop discipline and self-control, true psychological development also frees and expands us so that we can live richer, more fulfilling lives. Jung believed that when individuation is blocked, mental health problems ensue. C. G. Jung, "Problems of Modern Psychotherapy," in *The Practice of Psychotherapy*, ed. Herbert Read (New York: Bollingen, 1954).

3. George A. Morgan, Robert J. Harmon, and Christine A. Maslin-Cole, "Mastery Motivation: Definition and Measurement," *Early Education and Development* 1, no. 5 (1990).

4. Andrew J. Elliot, "Approach and Avoidance Motivation and Achievement Goals," *Educational Psychologist* 34, no. 3 (1999); R. W. White, "Motivation Reconsidered: The Concept of Competence," *Psychological Review* 66 (1959).

5. Robert Wright, *Nonzero: The Logic of Human Destiny* (New York: Pantheon Books, 2000).

6. This is by no means an original idea, but you can find recent scientific support and guidance for living it in chapter 10 of my book, *I'm Working on It in Therapy: How to Get the Most Out of Psychotherapy* (New York: Skyhorse, 2015).

7. Carol Dweck, *Mindset: The New Psychology of Success* (New York: Ballantine, 2006).

8. Gordon L. Flett, Paul L. Hewitt, Kirk R. Blankstein, and Shawn W. Mosher, "Perfectionism, Self-Actualization, and Personal Adjustment," *Journal of Social Behavior and Personality* 6, no. 5 (1991).

9. David Brooks, "The Strange Failure of the Educated Elite," *New York Times*, May 29, 2018.

Chapter 14: Support for the Compulsive's Journey

1. For a description of how therapy actually works, and specifically what you can do to make your therapy effective, see my book, *I'm Working on It in Therapy: How to Get the Most Out of Psychotherapy* (New York: Skyhorse, 2015).

2. Jonathan Shedler, "The Efficacy of Psychodynamic Psychotherapy," *American Psychologist* 65, no. 2 (2010): 98–109.

3. Christiane Steinert, Thomas Munder, Sven Rabung, Jürgen Hoyer, and Falk Leichsenring, "Psychodynamic Therapy: As Efficacious as Other Empirically Supported Treatments? A Meta-Analysis Testing Equivalence of Outcomes," *American Journal of Psychiatry* 174, no. 10 (2017); M. B. Connolly

Gibbons, R. Gallop, D. Thompson, D. Luther, K. Crits-Christoph, J. Jacobs, S. Yin, and P. Crits-Christoph, "Comparative Effectiveness of Cognitive Therapy and Dynamic Psychotherapy for Major Depressive Disorder in a Community Mental Health Setting: A Randomized Clinical Noninferiority Trial," *JAMA Psychiatry* 73, no. 1 (2016).

4. For introductory material you can visit https://www.insightmeditation.org or download the Insight Timer app.

5. Thich Nhat Hanh teaches a very simple and peaceful approach to meditation, which at the same time encourages an awareness of the larger world. You can find more about him and his approach at https://plumvillage.org/mindfulness-practice.

6. You can find more about MBSR at http://www.mindfullivingprograms.com/mbsr_background.php.

Chapter 15: Support and Suggestions for the Compulsive's Partner

1. N. M. Cain, E. B. Ansell, H. B. Simpson, and A. Pinto, "Interpersonal Functioning in Obsessive-Compulsive Personality Disorder," *Journal of Personality Assessment* 97, no. 1 (2015): 90–99, doi: 10.1080/00223891.2014.934376.

Afterword

1. C. G. Jung and S. Shamdasani, eds., *The Red Book: Liber Novus*, trans. M. Kyburz and J. Peck (New York: Norton, 2009), 395.

2. Ap Dijksterhuis, "Think Different: The Merits of Unconscious Thought in Preference Development and Decision Making," *Journal of Personality and Social Psychology* 87, no. 5 (2004).

~

Bibliography

Andreassen, C. S. "Workaholism: An Overview and Current Status of the Research." *Journal of Behavioral Addictions* 3, no. 1 (2014): 1–11.

Andreassen, C. S., M. D. Griffiths, J. Hetland, and S. Pallesen. "Development of a Work Addiction Scale." *Scandinavian Journal of Psychology* 53, no. 3 (2012): 265–72.

Ansari, Zohreh, and Javad Salehi Fadardi. "Enhanced Visual Performance in Obsessive Compulsive Personality Disorder." *Scandinavian Journal of Psychology* 57, no. 6 (2016): 542–46.

Backman, Fredrik. *A Man Called Ove: A Novel.* New York: Atria Books, 2014.

Baikie, Karen A., and Kay Wilhelm. "Emotional and Physical Health Benefits of Expressive Writing." *Advances in Psychiatric Treatment* 11, no. 5 (2005): 338–46.

Barber, J. P. "Change in Obsessive-Compulsive and Avoidant Personality Disorders Following Time-Limited Supportive Expressive Therapy." *Psychotherapy* 34, no. 2 (1997).

Beck, Melinda. "Inside the Minds of the Perfectionists: Researchers Used to Blame Parenting but Studies Suggest a Genetic Link; Procrastination Is a Problem." *Wall Street Journal*, October 29, 2012.

Berkowitz, Bonnie, and Clark Patterson. "The Health Hazards of Sitting." *Washington Post*, January 20, 2014.

Brooks, David. "The Strange Failure of the Educated Elite." *New York Times*, May 29, 2018.

Brown, Stuart, and Christopher Vaughan. *Play: How It Shapes the Brain, Opens the Imagination, and Invigorates the Soul*. New York: Penguin, 2010.

Cain, N. M., E. B. Ansell, H. B. Simpson, and A. Pinto. "Interpersonal Functioning in Obsessive-Compulsive Personality Disorder." *Journal of Personality Assessment* 97, no. 1 (2015): 90–99.

Cammer, Leonard. *Freedom from Compulsion: How to Liberate Yourself from the Uptight, Obsessive Patterns of Living That Rob You of Peace of Mind*. New York: Simon and Schuster, 1976.

Caplan, R. D., and K. W. Jones. "Effects of Work Load, Role Ambiguity, and Type A Personality on Anxiety, Depression, and Heart Rate." *Journal of Applied Psychology* 60, no. 6 (1975): 713–19.

Clifford, Christine, Robin Murray, and D. W. Fulker. "Genetic and Environmental Influences on Obsessional Traits and Symptoms." *Psychological Medicine* 14, no. 4 (1984). doi:10.1017/S0033291700019760

Connolly, E. J., and K. M. Beaver. "Examining the Genetic and Environmental Influences on Self-Control and Delinquency: Results from a Genetically Informative Analysis of Sibling Pairs." *Journal of Interpersonal Violence* 29, no. 4 (2014): 707–35.

Connolly Gibbons, M. B., R. Gallop, D. Thompson, D. Luther, K. Crits-Christoph, J. Jacobs, S. Yin, and P. Crits-Christoph. "Comparative Effectiveness of Cognitive Therapy and Dynamic Psychotherapy for Major Depressive Disorder in a Community Mental Health Setting: A Randomized Clinical Noninferiority Trial." *JAMA Psychiatry* 73, no. 1 (2016), 904–11.

Corballis, Michael C. *The Wandering Mind: What the Brain Does When You're Not Looking*. Chicago: University of Chicago Press, 2015.

Damasio, Antonio R. *Descartes' Error: Emotion, Reason, and the Human Brain*. London: Penguin, 2005.

Deci, Edward L., and Richard M. Ryan. "The 'What' and 'Why' of Goal Pursuits: Human Needs and the Self-Determination of Behavior." *Psychological Inquiry* 11, no. 4 (2000): 227–68.

de Manzano, O., S. Cervenka, A. Jucaite, O. Hellenas, L. Farde, and F. Ullen. "Individual Differences in the Proneness to Have Flow Experiences Are Linked to Dopamine D2-Receptor Availability in the Dorsal Striatum." *Neuroimage* 67 (2013): 1–6.

Devanand, D. P., et al. "Personality Disorders in Elderly Patients with Dysthymic Disorder." *American Journal of Geriatric Psychiatry* 8, no. 3 (2000): 188–95.

Diaconu, G., and G. Turecki. "Obsessive-Compulsive Personality Disorder and Suicidal Behavior: Evidence for a Positive Association in a Sample of Depressed Patients." *Journal of Clinical Psychiatry* 70, no. 11 (2009): 1551–56.

Di Domenico, S. I., and R. M. Ryan. "The Emerging Neuroscience of Intrinsic Motivation: A New Frontier in Self-Determination Research." *Frontiers in Human Neuroscience* 11 (2017): 145.

Diedrich, A., and U. Voderholzer. "Obsessive-Compulsive Personality Disorder: A Current Review." *Current Psychiatry Reports* 17, no. 2 (2015). doi: 10.1007/s11920-014-0547-8

Dijksterhuis, Ap. "Think Different: The Merits of Unconscious Thought in Preference Development and Decision Making." *Journal of Personality and Social Psychology* 87, no. 5 (2004): 586–98.

Dweck, Carol. *Mindset: The New Psychology of Success.* New York: Ballantine, 2006.

Elliot, Andrew J. "Approach and Avoidance Motivation and Achievement Goals." *Educational Psychologist* 34, no. 3 (1999): 169–89.

Elliot, Andrew J., and Marcy A. Church. "A Hierarchical Model of Approach and Avoidance Achievement Motivation." *Journal of Personality and Social Psychology* 72, no. 1 (1997): 218–32.

Flett, Gordon L., Paul L. Hewitt, Kirk R. Blankstein, and Shawn W. Mosher. "Perfectionism, Self-Actualization, and Personal Adjustment." *Journal of Social Behavior and Personality* 6, no. 5 (1991): 147–60.

Frost, Randy O., Gail Steketee, Leslie Cohn, and Kristine Griess. "Personality Traits in Subclinical and Non-Obsessive-Compulsive Volunteers and Their Parents." *Behaviour Research and Therapy* 32, no. 1 (1994): 47–56.

Gallwey, W. Timothy. *The Inner Game of Tennis.* New York: Random House, 1974.

Gendlin, Eugene. *Focusing.* 2nd Edition. New York: Bantam, 1982.

Gershoff, Elizabeth Thompson. "Corporal Punishment by Parents and Associated Child Behaviors and Experiences: A Meta-Analytic and Theoretical Review." *Psychological Bulletin* 128, no. 4 (2002): 539–79.

Gilbert, Daniel Todd. *Stumbling on Happiness.* New York: Knopf, 2006.

Gjerde, L. C., N. Czajkowski, E. Roysamb, E. Ystrom, K. Tambs, S. H. Aggen, R. E. Orstavik, et al. "A Longitudinal, Population-Based Twin Study of Avoidant and Obsessive-Compulsive Personality Disorder Traits from Early to Middle Adulthood." *Psychological Medicine* 45, no. 16 (2015): 3539–48.

Grant, J. E., M. N. Potenza, A. Weinstein, and D. A. Gorelick. "Introduction to Behavioral Addictions." *American Journal of Drug and Alcohol Abuse* 36, no. 5 (2010): 233–41.

Grant, Jon E., Marc E. Mooney, and Matt G. Kushner. "Prevalence, Correlates, and Comorbidity of DSM-IV Obsessive-Compulsive Personality Disorder: Results from the National Epidemiologic Survey on Alcohol and Related Conditions." *Journal of Psychiatric Research* 46, no. 4 (2012): 469–75.

Griffiths, M. D. "A 'Components' Model of Addiction within a Biopsychosocial Framework." *Journal of Substance Use* 10 (2005): 191–97.

———. "Workaholism Is Still a Useful Construct." *Addiction Research and Theory* 13 (2005): 97–100.

Griffiths, M. D., and M. Karanika-Murray. "Contextualising Over-Engagement in Work: Towards a More Global Understanding of Workaholism as an Addiction." *Journal of Behavioral Addictions* 1, no. 3 (2012): 87–95.

Gyurkovics, M., E. Kotyuk, E. R. Katonai, E. Z. Horvath, A. Vereczkei, and A. Szekely. "Individual Differences in Flow Proneness Are Linked to a Dopamine D2 Receptor Gene Variant." *Consciousness and Cognition* 42 (2016): 1–8.

Halmi, K. A., et al. "The Relation among Perfectionism, Obsessive-Compulsive Personality Disorder and Obsessive-Compulsive Disorder in Individuals with Eating Disorders." *International Journal of Eating Disorders* 38, no. 4 (2005): 371–74.

Helgeson, V. S. "Relation of Agency and Communion to Well-Being: Evidence and Potential Explanations." *Psychological Bulletin* 116, no. 3 (1994): 412–28.

Hummelen, B., T. Wilberg, G. Pedersen, and S. Karterud. "The Quality of the *DSM-IV* Obsessive-Compulsive Personality Disorder Construct as a Prototype Category." *Journal of Nervous and Mental Disease* 196, no. 6 (June 2008): 446–55.

Iranzo-Tatay, C., N. Gimeno-Clemente, M. Barbera-Fons, M. A. Rodriguez-Campayo, L. Rojo-Bofill, L. Livianos-Aldana, L. Beato-Fernandez, F. Vaz-Leal, and L. Rojo-Moreno. "Genetic and Environmental Contributions to Perfectionism and Its Common Factors." *Psychiatry Research* 230, no. 3 (2015): 932–39.

Jang, K. L., W. J. Livesley, and P. A. Vernon. "Heritability of the Big Five Personality Dimensions and Their Facets: A Twin Study." *Journal of Personality* 64, no. 3 (1996).

Johnson, Robert A. *Inner Work: Using Dreams and Active Imagination for Personal Growth.* San Francisco: Harper & Row, 1986.

Johnson, Stephen M. *Character Styles.* New York: Norton, 1994.

Jung, C. G. "Problems of Modern Psychotherapy." In *The Practice of Psychotherapy*, edited by Herbert Read. New York: Bollingen, 1954.

———. "Some Crucial Points in Psychoanalysis." In *Freud and Psychoanalysis*, edited by Edith Eder. New York: Bollingen, 1916.

Jung, C. G., and Shamdasani, S., eds. *The Red Book: Liber Novus.* Translated by M. Kyburz and J. Peck. New York: Norton, 2009.

Kendall, Joshua C. *America's Obsessives: The Compulsive Energy That Built a Nation.* New York: Grand Central Publishing, 2013.

Kulish, N. "Precocious Ego Development and Obsessive Compulsive Neurosis." *Journal of American Academy of Psychoanalysis* 16, no. 2 (1988): 167–87.

Mancebo, Maria C., Jane L. Eisen, Jon E. Grant, and Steven A. Rasmussen. "Obsessive Compulsive Personality Disorder and Obsessive Compulsive Disorder: Clinical Characteristics, Diagnostic Difficulties, and Treatment." *Annals of Clinical Psychiatry* 17, no. 4 (2005): 197–204.

Maslach, Christina, Wilmar B. Schaufeli, and Michael P. Leiter. "Job Burnout." *Annual Review of Psychology* 52 (2001): 397–422.

Matthews, K. A. "Matters of the Heart: Advancing Psychological Perspectives on Cardiovascular Diseases." *Perspectives on Psychological Science* 8, no. 6 (2013): 676–78.

McWilliams, Nancy. *Psychoanalytic Diagnosis: Understanding Personality Structure in the Clinical Process.* 2nd Edition. New York: Guilford Press, 2011.

Millon, Theodore. *Disorders of Personality: DSM-III, Axis II.* New York: Wiley, 1981.

Morgan, George A., Robert J. Harmon, and Christine A. Maslin-Cole. "Mastery Motivation: Definition and Measurement." *Early Education and Development* 1, no. 5 (1990): 318–39.

Nordahl, Hans M., and Tore Stiles. "Perceptions of Parental Bonding in Patients with Various Personality Disorders, Lifetime Depressive Disorders, and Healthy Controls." *Journal of Personality Disorders* 11, no. 4 (1997): 391–402.

Nutt, Amy Ellis, with Frances E. Jensen. *The Teenage Brain: A Neuroscientist's Survival Guide to Raising Adolescents and Young Adults.* New York: HarperCollins, 2015.

Orpen, Christopher. "Type A Personality as a Moderator of the Effects of Role Conflict, Role Ambiguity and Role Overload on Individual Strain." *Journal of Human Stress* 8, no. 2 (1982): 8–14.

Pang, Alex Soojung-Kim. *Rest: Why You Get More Done When You Work Less.* New York: Basic Books, 2016.

Panksepp, J. "Emotional Endophenotypes in Evolutionary Psychiatry." *Progress in Neuro-Psychopharmacology and Biological Psychiatry* 30, no. 5 (2006): 774–84.

Pedersen, Nancy L., et al. "Genetic and Environmental Influences for Type A-Like Measures and Related Traits: A Study of Twins Reared Apart and Twins Reared Together." *Psychosomatic Medicine* 51 (1989): 428–40.

Piazza, Pier Vincenzo, and Michel Le Moal. "Glucocorticoids as a Biological Substrate of Reward: Physiological and Pathophysiological Implications." *Brain Research Reviews* 25, no. 3 (1997): 359–72.

Pinto, A., J. E. Steinglass, A. L. Greene, E. U. Weber, and H. B. Simpson. "Capacity to Delay Reward Differentiates Obsessive-Compulsive Disorder and Obsessive-Compulsive Personality Disorder." *Biological Psychiatry* 75, no. 8 (2014): 653–59.

Reich, Wilhelm. *Character-Analysis*. 3rd, enl. ed. New York: Orgone Institute Press, 1949.

Reus, Rob J. M., and Paul M. G. Emmelkamp. "Obsessive–Compulsive Personality Disorder: A Review of Current Empirical Findings." *Personality and Mental Health* 6, no. 1 (2012): 1–21.

Rimfeld, Kaili, Yulia Kovas, Philip S. Dale, and Robert Plomin. "True Grit and Genetics: Predicting Academic Achievement from Personality." *Journal of Personality and Social Psychology*, 111, no. 5 (2016).

Rottenberg, Jonathan. *The Depths: The Evolutionary Origins of the Depression Epidemic*. New York: Basic Books, 2014.

Samuel, D. B., and T. A. Widiger. "Conscientiousness and Obsessive-Compulsive Personality Disorder." *Personality Disorders: Theory, Research, and Treatment* 2, no. 3 (2011): 161–74.

Shadick, Nancy A., et al. "A Randomized Controlled Trial of an Internal Family Systems-Based Psychotherapeutic Intervention on Outcomes in Rheumatoid Arthritis: A Proof-of-Concept Study." *Journal of Rheumatology* 40, no. 11 (2013).

Shafran, Roz, and Warren Mansell. "Perfectionism and Psychopathology: A Review of Research and Treatment." *Clinical Psychology Review* 21, no. 6 (2001): 879–906.

Shamay-Tsoory, S. G., N. Adler, J. Aharon-Peretz, D. Perry, and N. Mayseless. "The Origins of Originality: The Neural Bases of Creative Thinking and Originality." *Neuropsychologia* 49, no. 2 (2011): 178–85.

Shedler, Jonathan. "The Efficacy of Psychodynamic Psychotherapy." *American Psychologist* 65, no. 2 (2010): 98–109.

Simonson, Itamar, and Aner Sela. "On the Heritability of Consumer Decision Making: An Exploratory Approach for Studying Genetic Effects on Judgment and Choice." *Journal of Consumer Research* 37, no. 6 (2011): 951–66.

Smallwood, J., and J. Andrews-Hanna. "Not All Minds That Wander Are Lost: The Importance of a Balanced Perspective on the Mind-Wandering State." *Frontiers in Psychology* 4 (2013): 441.

Steenkamp, Maria M., Michael K. Suvak, Benjamin D. Dickstein, M. Tracie Shea, and Brett T. Litz. "Emotional Functioning in Obsessive-Compulsive Personality Disorder: Comparison to Borderline Personality Disorder and Healthy Controls." *Journal of Personality Disorders* 29, no. 6 (2015): 1–15.

Steinert, Christiane, Thomas Munder, Sven Rabung, Jürgen Hoyer, and Falk Leichsenring. "Psychodynamic Therapy: As Efficacious as Other Empirically Supported Treatments? A Meta-Analysis Testing Equivalence of Outcomes." *American Journal of Psychiatry* 174, no. 10 (2017): 943–53.

Torgersen, S., et al. "A Twin Study of Personality Disorders." *Comprehensive Psychiatry* 41, no. 6 (2000): 416–25.

Trosclair, Gary. *I'm Working on It in Therapy: How to Get the Most Out of Psychotherapy.* New York: Skyhorse, 2015.

van Grootheest, D. S., M. Bartels, C. E. van Beijsterveldt, D. C. Cath, A. T. Beekman, J. J. Hudziak, and D. I. Boomsma. "Genetic and Environmental Contributions to Self-Report Obsessive-Compulsive Symptoms in Dutch Adolescents at Ages 12, 14, and 16." *Journal of the American Academy of Child and Adolescent Psychiatry* 47, no. 10 (2008): 1182–88.

Villemarette-Pittman, Nicole R., et al. "Obsessive-Compulsive Personality Disorder and Behavioral Disinhibition." *Journal of Psychology* 138, no. 1 (2004): 5–22.

Weinberg, George H. *Invisible Masters: Compulsions and the Fear That Drives Them.* New York: Grove Press, 1993.

Weiner, Eric. *The Geography of Bliss: One Grump's Search for the Happiest Places in the World.* New York: Twelve/Hachette, 2008.

White, R. W. "Motivation Reconsidered: The Concept of Competence." *Psychological Review* 66 (1959): 297–333.

Widiger, T. A., and G. T. Smith. "Personality and Psychopathology." In *Handbook of Personality: Theory and Research*, edited by O. P. John, R. W. Robins, and L. A. Pervin, 743–69. New York: Guilford Press, 2008.

Wilson, Edward O. *The Meaning of Human Existence.* New York: Liveright Publishing Corporation, a division of W. W. Norton & Company, 2014.

Wright, Robert. *Nonzero: The Logic of Human Destiny.* New York: Pantheon Books, 2000.

Index

action, 43; Adult character and, 79; Baez on, 79; choice of, 44; Frank and, 80–81; Gandhi on, 79; summary on, 82–83

active imagination, Jung on, 192n9

addictions: to behaviors, 38, 108; compulsions and, 23; cortisol and endorphins impact on, 38. *See also* work addiction

adolescent, OCPD symptoms in, 22

Adult character, 52, 52–53, 53, 72; action and, 79; direction for, 68; recognition loss of, 67

aggression, 61, 90, 171, 194n1. *See also* passive-aggressive behavior

ambition: God of, 54; inborn character trait of, 28

American Psychiatric Association (APA), on OCPD, 16

Americans with Disabilities Act, 191n1

anger: compulsive urge and, 4, 74; dangers of, 61–62; Doris and, 88; of Frank, 61–62, 69, 70; hate and outbursts of, 62; of Parent character, 66–67; Pimentel on, 59; reasons for, 61

Antoine (client): on time and money, 95–97, 100–102; vulnerability of, 100

anxiety, 2, 63–64, 176; avoidance reinforcement of, 37–38, 56; dreams, 66; OCD and, 21, 22; over moral standards and productivity, 63; of parents, 30, 35

APA. *See* American Psychiatric Association

appearance, parents emphasis on, 31, 35–36

approach behaviors, 189n21

As Good as It Gets (film), 174–75

attachments, secure, 31

avoidance: anxiety reinforced by, 37–38, 56; behaviors, 189n21; of division of labor, 172–74, 195n3; of emotions, 63, 70, 191n2; procrastination and emotion, 63; in work and career, 111–12

Baez, Joan, 79
Barber, Jacques, 75
behavioral changes, 11, 49
behaviors: addiction to, 38, 108; approach and avoidance, 189n21; hoarding, 17, 18, 22, 96, 99–100; passive-aggressive, 61–62, 189n22; repetitive, 3, 21; seeking, 28; self-determined, 28
Berg, A. Scott, 133
Bergen Work Addiction Scale (BWAS), 108
body: dangers for, 89–91; Doris and, 87–88, 91–92; exercise of, 90, 91; heart disease, 90; opportunities and, 88–89; relaxation of, 89, 93; sex and, 89, 90–91, 92; summary on, 93
boundary setting, communication for, 171
brain scans, on OCPD, 28
Brooks, David, 148
Brother character, of Frank, 81
Brown, Stuart, 135
burnout, in work and career, 111
BWAS. See Bergen Work Addiction Scale

Cammer, Leonard, 23–24
Campbell, Joseph, 179
CBT. See cognitive behavioral therapy

challenging experiences, flow and, 187n12
change: behavioral and internal, 11; effort in, 8; emotions as element of, 60; Lilly perception of, 167–68; methods for emotion, 44; through relationships, 155
chaotic family, 30, 34–35
characteristics, of driven personality, 5, 11
characters in story, insight on, 51–54
Child character, 52, 52–53, 53, 57; desire, hope, excitement of, 66; of Frank, 70, 81
childhood: fear, 6, 7; OCD symptoms in, 22
children: compulsive urge and fearful, 6–7, 8; driven personality and fear of, 6–7; insecurity situations for, 30–31, 33; resilience of, 36
cognitive behavioral therapy (CBT), 157, 158
communication: boundary setting, 171; of needs, 169; in partner support, 168–72; therapy encouragement, 170–71; timing for, 169–70
completion, George's need for, 3
compulsions: addictions and, 23; defined, 22; Freud on, 189n22; rigid strategies for, 50
compulsive personality: counting and, 19; maintenance impact on, 36–39; OCPD compared to, 21–23
compulsive urge: connections with sources in, 7–9; conscious control of, 4; driven personality and, 5–6; beyond external need, 3;

fear and anger in, 4, 74; fearful
child and, 6–7, 8; hero or heroine
healthy, 4; personal story for,
9–10; relationships impacted by,
3; response to, 4
concentration, 20, 28; meditation as,
160–61
connections: emotions and
character, 68–70; with sources, in
compulsive urge, 7–9
conscientiousness, 29
conscious control, of compulsive
urge, 4
consciousness, 59–60, 71, 89
control: conscious, of compulsive
urge, 4; Jung on, 179; needs and
plan to, 2–3; sharing of, 179–80
coping: driven personality impacted
by, 11; of George, 36; personality
development and strategy for,
32–36; of Sharon, 36
cortisol, addictions impacted by, 38
counting, compulsive personality
and, 19
couples therapy, 91, 158, 165
criticism: in driven personality, 5;
by parents, 30, 34, 188n16; self-,
147–48
cultivation, of meaning, 73–78
culture: OCPD sanction of, 32;
parental aspect of, 32

Damasio, Anthony, 66
dangers: of anger, 61–62; for body,
89–91; for people, 120–22; in
psychological growth, 145–46; of
rest and play, 136–37; of time and
money, 98–100; work and career,
108–13
Darwin, Charles, 95

Davis, Bette, 105
Deci, Edward L., 193n1
delegation: George and, 18; in
OCPD, 16
depression, 62; of Doris, 88; of
George, 1; OCPD, suicide and,
19
Descartes, René, 66
Descartes' Error (Damasio), 66
desire, 65, 75; of Child character, 66;
obligation overriding of, 19
determination: on guard feeling and,
2; of Hero character, 67
devices, rest and play impacted by,
137
Diedrich, Alice, 185n1
direction: for Adult character, 68;
from emotions, 65–66
discontent, 64–65
displacement, in psychological
growth, 146–47
distress, of George, 1
division of labor, avoidance of,
172–74, 195n3
dopamine, 187n12
Doris (client): anger and, 88; body
and, 87–88, 91–92; depression
of, 88
dreams: anxiety, 66; of Frank, 57;
insight and, 55, 57; life story
characters and, 55
driven personality: characteristics of,
5, 11; childhood fear and, 6–7;
compulsive urge and, 5–6; coping
impact on, 11; criticism and, 5;
efficiency in, 19; environment
impact on, 11; of George, 5–8;
nature impact on, 11; security
need in, 6; of Sharon, 25–27
Dryden, John, 25

DSM-5 criteria, for OCPD, 16–17
Dubliners (Joyce), 89

efficiency, in driven personality, 19
effort, in change, 8
Emerson, Ralph Waldo, 99
emotions: anger, 4, 59, 61–62,
    69, 70, 74, 88; anxiety, 2, 21,
    22, 30, 35, 37–38, 55, 63–64,
    66, 176; avoidance of, 63, 70,
    191n2; change as element of,
    60; character connections,
    68–70; depression, 1, 19, 62, 88;
    desire, 19, 65, 66, 75; direction
    from, 65–66; discontent, 64–65;
    experience of, 59–66; fear, 4, 6–8,
    22, 63–64, 70, 74, 99; of Frank,
    61, 68–70; healthy compulsion
    steps on, 43, 44; identification
    of, 71; journaling and, 60; layers
    of, 60–61; methods to change,
    44; OCPD cycle of negative, 60;
    parents disapproval of, 30, 34;
    Pimentel on, 59; procrastination,
    63; of sadness, powerlessness,
    futility, 62; shame and guilt,
    62–63, 69, 70; summary on,
    70–72; wisdom and direction
    from, 65–66
endorphins, addiction impacted by,
    38
environment: driven personality
    impacted by, 11; of George, 31;
    peer groups in, 32; personality
    development and, 30–32, 34–35;
    of Sharon, 31
escape fantasies, 19; of George, 1–2
excitement, of Child character, 66
exercise, 90, 91
experience, of emotions, 59–66

external achievements, psychological
    growth and, 146–47

family: as chaotic, 30, 34–35;
    of George, 31; personality
    development and, 11, 30–32,
    34–35; of Sharon, 31
fear, 63–64; of child, 6–8;
    compulsive urge and, 4, 74; of
    Frank, 70; OCD contamination,
    22; in time and money, 99
fixation of fixing, 20
flow, challenging experiences and,
    187n12
Frank (client): action and, 80–81;
    anger of, 61–62, 69, 70; Brother
    character of, 81; Child character
    of, 70, 81; dreams of, 57;
    emotions of, 61, 68–70; fear of,
    70; healthy compulsion steps for,
    45–47; Hercules character of,
    56–57, 76; Hero character of, 68;
    insight and, 55–57; meaning and,
    76–78; Parent character of, 56,
    57, 70, 76, 81; Prophet character
    of, 56–57, 70, 76, 81; resentment
    of, 69; shame and guilt of, 69, 70;
    vulnerability of, 69
Freud, Sigmund, 189n22
Fromm, Erich, 117
frugality, 96
futility, 62

Gallwey, Timothy, 135, 143, 144,
    146, 178–79
Gandhi, Mohandas, 79
gender roles, Helgeson on, 195n3
genes. *See* nature
genetic predisposition, 28, 185n1.
    See also nature

George (client): compulsive personality maintenance of, 38–39; coping of, 36; delegation and, 18; depression and distress of, 1; driven personality of, 5–8; escape fantasies of, 1–2; family and environment of, 31; moral standards of, 17; nature, in personality development of, 29; OCPD and, 17–18; perfectionism in, 17; productivity habit of, 3; rules and, 17–18; sense of mission of, 2; trapped feeling of, 2
Gilbert, Daniel, 63
goal-directed behavior, 28
goals, meaning and, 74–76
God of ambition, 54
grievance, 188n15
group therapy, 158–59

habits: Dryden on, 15; George productivity, 3
hate, anger and, 62
healthy compulsion: action step for, 43, 44, 79–83; emotion step for, 43, 44; of Frank, 45–47; insight step for, 43–44, 49–57; meaning step for, 43, 44, 73–78; world role, sharing control and, 179–80
heart disease, 90
Helgeson, Vicki, 195n3
Hercules character, 67, 145; of Frank, 56–57, 76
Hero character: determination of, 67; of Frank, 68
hero or heroine, healthy compulsive urge of, 4
hoarding behavior, 96; OCD, 22; OCPD, 17, 18; for time and money, 99–100

hope, of Child character, 66
Hosseini, Khaled, 4
humor, 139

idealism, 19
identification: of emotions, 71; of insight, 43–44
imagination, 75; characters use for, 67; Jung on active, 192n9
impatience, relationships and, 99
inborn character traits: ambition, 28; concentration, 20, 28; conscientiousness, 29; goal-directed behavior, 28; moral indignation, 29; motivation to master skills, 28; perfectionism, 28; perseverance, 28; prudence, 29; seeking behavior, 28; self-determined behavior, 28; self-restraint, 28
individual psychotherapy, 155, 165; CBT, 157, 158; partner encouragement of, 170–71; psychoanalytic therapy, 157; psychodynamic therapy, 157, 158; trust in, 156; through videoconferencing, 159
individuation, 143
Inner Game, of Gallwey, 144, 146, 178–79
insecure: relationships, OCPD and, 34; situations for child, 30–31, 33
insight: on characters in story, 51–54; on compulsion motivation, 49–50; dreams and, 55, 57; Frank and, 55–57; into God of ambition, 54; identification of, 43–44; security and, 50–51; summary on, 57
internal changes, 11

Internal Family Systems, of Schwartz, 192n9
intrinsic motivation, 189n21; neuroscience of, 194n7
intrusive parents, 30
intrusive thoughts, 3

Jill (client), work addiction of, 105–7, 113–15
Jobs, Steve, 4
Johnson, Stephen, 192n1
journaling, emotions and, 60
Joyce, James, 89
Judge character, 75–76
judgment, 10, 77; of Parent character, 66–67
Jung, Carl, 135; active imagination of, 192n9; on control, 179; on individuation, 143, 196n2; on neurosis, 74; on self-development, 141; on self-realization, 183n3

layers, of emotions, 60–61
Lilly (client): partner support by, 163–64; perception of change of, 167–68
love, Fromm on, 117

MacWilliams, Nancy, 91
maintenance, in compulsive personality, 11; of George, 38–39; in personality development, 36–39; of Sharon, 39
Maslow, A. H., 196n1
mastery motivation, 187n9
The Matrix (film), 5–6
MBSR. See Mindfulness Based Stress Reduction
meaning, 43, 44; cultivation of, 73–78; Frank and, 76–78; goals and, 74–76; nature and, 74

meditation, 160; MBSR, 161, 198n6; Vipassana Meditation, 161
Meredith (client), rest and play of, 133–34, 138–39
mindfulness, 160–61
Mindfulness Based Stress Reduction (MBSR), 161, 198n6
moral indignation, 188n15
moral standards, 20; anxiety over, 63; of George, 17; in OCPD, 16
Morgan, George A., 187n9
motivation: insight on compulsion, 49–50; intrinsic, 189n21, 194n7; to master skills, 28; Morgan on mastery, 187n9; nature and, 185nn9–10; Panksepp on nature and, 187n10; for psychological growth, 145
The Music Within (film), 191n1

nature, in personality development, 11, 185n1; of George, 29; meaning and, 74; moral indignation and grievance, 188n15; motivation and, 187nn9–10; OCPD brain scans on, 28; of Sharon, 29; twin studies on, 28, 185n2
needs: communication of, 169; compulsive urge beyond external, 3; Deci and Ryan on, 193n1; George completion, 3; of plan to control, 2–3
neglect: in rest and play, 136; in work and career, 112
neuroscience, of intrinsic motivation, 194n7
neurosis, 4, 74

obligation, desire overridden by, 19
obsessions, defined, 22

obsessive-compulsive disorder
(OCD), 11; anxiety and, 21,
22; childhood symptoms of, 22;
contamination fear, 22; counting
and, 19; fixated on fixing in, 20;
goal completion urgency, 18;
hoarding behavior, 22; OCPD
compared to, 21–23, 185n8;
resolution and, 20; rituals and
checking of, 22
obsessive-compulsive personality
disorder (OCPD), 15; adolescent
symptoms of, 22; APA on, 16;
brain scans on, 28; Cammer
self-test for, 23–24; compulsive
personality compared to, 21–23;
cultural sanction of, 32; delegation
in, 16; Diedrich on genes and,
185n1; DSM-5 criteria for,
16–17; George and, 17–18;
healthy compulsive compared
to, 20–21; hoarding behavior
of, 17, 18; insecure relationships
and, 34; moral standards in,
16; negative emotions cycle of,
60; OCD compared to, 21–23,
185n8; perfectionism, 16, 194n1;
productivity in, 19; rigidity in, 17,
194n1; strengths of, 184n7; suicide,
depression and, 19; symptoms
diminishing for, 37; traits
associated with, 16, 18–20, 184n6
OCD. See obsessive-compulsive
disorder
OCPD. See obsessive-compulsive
personality disorder
on guard feeling, determination and,
2
online support groups, 175
opportunities: body and, 88–89; for
people, 119–20; for psychological

growth, 144–45; rest and play
and, 134–35; time and money
and, 97–98; work and career and,
107
overprotectiveness, of parents, 30, 35

Panksepp, Jaak, 187n10; on emotion
neurological networks, 193n2
Parent character, 52, 52–53, 53;
anger and judgment of, 66–67; of
Frank, 56, 57, 70, 76, 81
parenting, 126–27; summary on,
130–31; Ted and, 117–18,
128–29
parents: anxiety and neediness of,
30, 35; appearance emphasis
by, 31, 35–36; disappointing
relationships with, 30, 35;
disapproval of emotions
by, 30, 34; as intrusive, 30;
lack of standards of, 31, 35;
overprotectiveness of, 30, 35;
rigidity and criticism by, 30, 34,
188n16; security lack from, 30
partners, 124; summary on, 130–31;
Ted and, 117–18, 125–26. See
also support, for partner
passive-aggressive behavior, 61–62,
189n22
Pavarotti, Luciano, 15
peer groups, 32
people: dangers for, 120–22;
opportunities for, 119–20;
summary on, 130–31; Ted and,
117–18, 122–24
perception: appreciation of good,
166; emotions and, 167; Lilly
change of, 167–68; in partner
support, 166–68
perfectionism, 28; Barber on, 75; in
George, 17; in OCPD, 16, 194n1;

in psychological growth, 147–48; in rest and play, 136–37, 139; in work and career, 110–11

perseverance, 28

personality characters: of Adult, 52, 52–53, 53, 67, 68, 72, 79; of Brother, 81; of Child, 52, 52–53, 53, 57, 66, 70, 81; dominant figures in, 54; of Hercules, 56–57, 67, 76, 145; imagination use for, 67; of Judge, 75–76; of Parent, 52, 52–53, 53, 56, 57, 66–67, 70, 76, 81; of Prophet, 56–57, 70, 76, 81

personality development: coping strategy development and, 32–36; family, environment and, 11, 30–32, 34–35; maintenance compulsive personality in, 11, 36–39; nature and, 11, 28–29, 74, 185nn1–2, 187nn9–10, 188n15

Pimentel, Richard, 59, 191n1

Pinto, Anthony, 191n2

plan to control need, 2–3

powerlessness, 62

procrastination, emotion avoidance and, 63

productivity: anxiety over, 63; George habit of, 3; in OCPD, 19

Prophet character, of Frank, 56–57, 70, 76, 81

Protestant work ethic, 188n20

prudence, 29, 188n14

psychoanalytic therapy, 157

psychodynamic therapy: effectiveness of, 158; Shedler on, 157

psychological growth, 151; Cindy and, 141–42, 148–50; dangers in, 145–46; displacement in, 146–47; Dweck on, 145; external achievements and, 146–47;

instinct toward, 142–44; Jung on, 141; living in the future and, 147; motivation for, 145; opportunities for, 144–45; perfectionism and self-criticism, 147–48; religion and, 147; self-preoccupation, 148

punishment, 10

quality standards, for work and career, 20

reasons, for anger, 61

Reasons for Living Inventory, 19

recognition, Adult character loss of, 67

Reich, Wilhelm, 19

relationships: change through, 155; commitment to, 20; compulsive urge impact on, 3; impatience and, 99; OCPD and insecure, 34; parents disappointing, 30, 35; partner support and improvement in, 164–66

relaxation: of body, 89, 93; in rest and play, 139

religion, 177–78; psychological growth and, 147

repetitive behaviors, 3, 21

research, on work addiction, 109

resentment, of Frank, 69

resilience, of children, 36

resolution, 20

response, to compulsive urge, 4

rest and play: approach to, 135; Berg on, 133; Brown on, 135; dangers of, 136–37; devices and, 137; Meredith and, 133–34, 138–39; neglect and, 136; opportunities and, 134–35; perfectionism and,

136–37, 139; relaxation in, 139;
summary on, 139
rigidity, 77; in OCPD, 17, 194n1; of
parents, 30, 34, 188n16; strategy,
for compulsion, 50
"The Role of Experiential
Avoidance in Obsessive-
Compulsive Personality Disorder
Traits" (Wheaton and Pinto),
191n2
Roshi, Suzuki, 73
rules, 7; George and, 17–18
Ryan, Richard M., 193n1

sadness, 62
Schwartz, Richard, 192n9
security, need for: in driven
personality, 6; insight on, 50–51;
parents and lack of, 30
seeking behavior, 28
self-actualization, 143; Maslow on,
196n1
self-care: characteristics
reinforcement, 174–75; division
of labor avoidance, 172–74,
195n3; for partner, 172–77;
partner support for, 175–76
self-criticism, psychological growth
and, 147–48
self-determined behavior, 28
self-esteem, 37–38; compensation
for, 49
self-esteem, compensation for, 49
self-help, 161–62
self-preoccupation, 148
self-restraint, 28
sense of mission, of George, 2
sex, 89–92
shame and guilt, 62–63; of Frank,
69, 70

Sharon (client): compulsive
personality maintenance
of, 39; coping of, 36; driven
personality of, 25–27; family and
environment of, 31; nature, in
personality development of, 29
Shedler, Jonathan, 157
standards: moral, 16, 17, 20, 63;
parents lack of, 31, 35; work
quality, 20
strategy, for work addiction, 50
strengths, of healthy compulsive:
efficiency, 20; focus and
concentration, 20; independent
work, 20; moral standards, 20;
thrift and conscious spending,
21; work and relationships
commitment, 20; work quality
standards, 20
strengths, of OCPD, 184n7
stress, 90
Stumbling on Happiness (Gilbert), 63
suicide, 4; OCPD , depression and,
19
summary: on action steps, 82–83; on
body, 93; on emotions, 70–72; on
insight, 57; on parenting, 130–31;
on partners, 130–31; on people,
130–31; on rest and play, 139; on
time and money, 102–3; on work
and career, 115–16
support, for partner: communication
in, 168–72; Lilly and, 163–64;
perception in, 166–68;
relationship improvement, 164–
66; self-care, 172–77
support, in compulsive's journey:
couples therapy, 91, 158, 165;
group therapy, 158–59; individual
psychotherapy, 155–58, 165,

170–71; meditation, 160–61; self-help, 161–62; support groups, 159–60, 175

support groups, 159–60; online, 175

sympathetic nervous system, 90, 93

symptoms, OCPD diminishing of, 37

Ted (client): parenting and, 117–18, 128–29; partners and, 117–18, 125–26; people and, 117–18, 122–24

therapy encouragement, communication of, 170–71

Thich Nhat Hanh, 161, 198n5

time and money: Antoine and, 95–97, 100–102; dangers of, 98–100; Darwin on, 95; Emerson on, 99; fear and, 99; hoarding of, 99–100; opportunities and, 97–98; sensitivity to, 97–98; summary on, 102–3

timing, for communication, 169–70

Tolstoy, Leo, 43

traits: compulsivity inheritance of, 28; inborn character, 28–29; of OCPD, 16, 18–20, 184n6

trapped feeling, of George, 2

trust, in individual psychotherapy, 156

twin studies, on nature, 28, 185n2

Type A personality, 90, 112, 185n2

Type B personality, 112

unrealistic expectations, 10

videoconferencing, 159

Vipassana Meditation, 161

vulnerability: of Antoine, 100; of Frank, 69

Watts, Alan, 105

Weinberg, George, 37

Weiner, Eric, 54

Wells, H. G., 25

Wheaton, Michael, 191n2

Wilson, Edward O., 49

wisdom, emotions as source of, 65–66

work addiction, 3, 17, 110, 191n1; BWAS, 108; of Jill, 105–7, 113–15; research on, 109; strategy for, 50

Workaholics Anonymous, 159

work and career: burnout, 111; dangers, 108–13; Davis on, 105; distraction and avoidance, 111–12; Jill and, 105–7, 113–15; neglect, 112; opportunities and, 107; perfectionism and, 110–11; quality standards for, 20; summary on, 115–16; Watts on, 105; work addiction, 3, 17, 50, 108–10, 113–15, 191n1

work ethic, Protestant, 188n20

world, sharing control in, 179–80

Wright, Richard, 25

yoga, 92, 93

~

About the Author

Gary Trosclair, DMA, LCSW, is a psychotherapist and Jungian analyst in private practice in New York City and Westchester County, New York. He is president of the New York Association for Analytical Psychology and serves on the faculty of the Jung Institute of New York, the Jung Foundation of New York, and the New York Center for Jungian Studies. He is the author of *I'm Working on It in Therapy: How to Get the Most Out of Psychotherapy* and of the blog *The Healthy Compulsive Project*. He lives in Tuckahoe, New York, with his wife and two daughters.